Editor
Mara Ellen Guckian

Editor in Chief
Brent L. Fox, M. Ed.

Creative Director
Sarah M. Fournier

Cover Artist
Sarah Kim

Illustrator
Mark Mason

Art Coordinator
Renée Mc Elwee

Imaging
Amanda R. Harter
Crystal-Dawn Keitz

Publisher
Mary D. Smith, M.S. Ed.

For standards correlations, visit
*http://www.teachercreated.com
/standards/*.

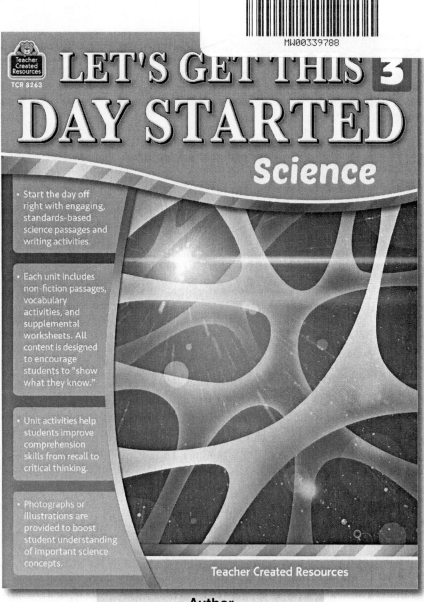

Author
Tracy Edmunds, M.A.

Teacher Created Resources
12621 Western Avenue
Garden Grove, CA 92841
www.teachercreated.com
ISBN: 978-1-4206-8263-2

© 2020 Teacher Created Resources
Made in U.S.A.

Table of Contents

Table of Contents *(cont.)*

Physical Science

Science and Engineering Practices

Introduction

Science is the study of the world around us. Students experience science every day without knowing it! Learning about how the world works can be fascinating, but sometimes, students must find fun and accessible science topics before they realize how enjoyable science can be. The passages in this book contain high-interest topics that will immediately hook students and challenge them to see science at work in their own experiences. From how to forecast the weather with dandelions to why farmers put magnets in cows, students will enjoy practicing their informational reading skills with interesting science topics.

This book is arranged into four sections:

Life Science   **Physical Science**
Earth and Space Science   **Science and Engineering Practices**

Within each section are a number of units, each of which explores an important science topic. Each unit comprises five pages. Most pages feature reading passages and response questions. Some pages include science-related worksheets. Within each science discipline, the units are sequential and build upon one another.

Teachers should not feel restricted by a daily warm-up activity. Sometimes, schedules change. A morning assembly, a make-up lesson, or just an extra-busy day can easily throw off the classroom schedule for days. A teacher never knows what his or her week is going to look like. *Let's Get This Day Started: Science* units do not need to be completed every day or even every other day. Teachers can take their time and arrange the activities to fit their own schedules. A teacher may choose to do a unit a week (one passage a day), or, at other times, spread a unit out over a few weeks. There is no right or wrong way.

These pages are meant to supplement, not substitute for, a science curriculum. Use them in conjunction with science lessons whenever possible.

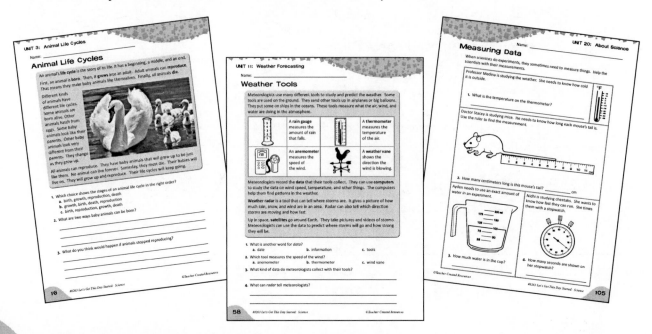

Name: _____

Lion Prides

Lions live in groups called **prides**. There are usually about 15 lions in a pride. Males, females, and cubs make up a pride. They live together, hunt together, and eat together. They take care of one another.

When lions hunt together, it is better for all of them. It is easier to catch prey when they help one another. And they are less likely to get hurt. The whole pride can scare away other animals that want to take their food.

The pride can protect the young cubs by working together. Mother lions care for and feed one another's cubs. The pride teaches the cubs to hunt.

1. What is a group of lions called? _____

2. Write two reasons lions live in *prides*.

   _____

   _____

   _____

3. If you were a lion, would you want to live in a *pride*?   **Yes**   **No**

   Why or why not?

   _____

   _____

   _____

Name: _____

Termite Homes

Termites are small insects. They eat wood and dead plants. They live in groups called **colonies**. Each colony has a queen, soldiers, and workers. They work together to protect one another. Termites live on every continent but Antarctica.

The worker termites build big nests to live in. Some dig tunnels under the ground for their nests. Other termite colonies build mounds out of mud. Some termite mounds are as tall as a house!

Many animals eat termites, such as ants, birds, frogs, and lizards. Chimpanzees push sticks into termite mounds to get the termites. Then, they eat the termites off the stick. It's like a termite lollipop!

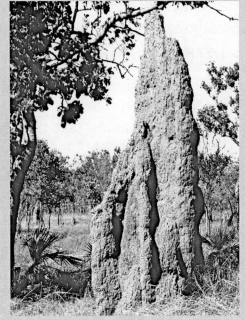

Termite mound

1. What are termites?

a. mammals

b. insects

c. birds

2. Name three kinds of termites in a *colony*.

_____

_____

_____

3. Why do termites work together?

_____

_____

_____

_____

_____

Name: _____

A Termite Colony

Each termite colony has a king and a queen. Only the queen lays eggs. She can lay up to 40,000 eggs in a day! Queens are much bigger than the other termites. Termite queens have the longest lives of any insect. They can live to be up to 50 years old!

The rest of the termites in the colony are workers or soldiers. Worker and soldier termites cannot fly. Most are blind. They use their antennae to touch, taste, and feel. Blind termites can communicate with one another by putting out special smells.

Termite colony

Worker termites build the nest. They also eat dead plants and wood. They digest the food and then feed it to other termites in the colony. Some workers take care of the nest and the young termites.

Soldier termites defend the colony. Some soldier termites have large heads and big jaws to fight off predators. Their jaws are so big that they cannot feed themselves. The workers have to feed them. Some soldier termites can shoot a sticky spray at enemies.

1. What does the queen do in the termite colony?
   a. builds her nest
   b. protects the nest
   c. lays the termite eggs

2. What are two ways worker termites help their colony?

   _____

   _____

3. Do you think one worker termite could survive on its own? Why, or why not?

   _____

   _____

   _____

Name: _____

Ring-tailed Lemur Groups

Ring-tailed lemurs are **primates**, a kind of mammal. This kind of lemur is about the size of a pet cat. The name comes from the black and white stripes on their long tails. Ring-tailed lemurs spend about half their time in the trees and half their time walking on the ground. They eat plants and insects. Ring-tailed lemurs live in groups called **troops**. A female lemur leads each group.

Group	Number of Lemurs
Miora	19
Linah	14
Ando	20
Hanitra	15
Antsa	17

A scientist is studying ring-tailed lemurs. She wants to know about the size of lemur troops. She observes some troops. She gives each troop leader a name. She counts and records the number of ring-tailed lemurs in each leader's group.

1. Use the scientist's data to complete this bar graph. The first one has been done for you.

Miora																				
Linah																				
Ando																				
Hanitra																				
Antsa																				

1 2 3 4 5 6 7 8 9 10 11 12 13 14 15 16 17 18 19 20

2. Which group had the most lemurs? _____

3. Which group had the fewest lemurs? _____

4. How many more lemurs did Ando's group have than Linah's group? _____

Name: _____

Why Animals Communicate

Animals can **communicate** with one another. This means they share information. Animals do this for many reasons.

Animals can communicate to defend themselves.

▶ Some animals have bright colors to show predators that they do not taste good.

▶ Some animals can make sounds to warn others of danger.

▶ Rattlesnakes shake their tails. This tells hawks and coyotes not to eat them. The hawks and coyotes do not want to get bitten!

Animals can communicate to find food.

▶ Bees do a special dance to show other bees where the best flowers are.

▶ Ants leave a trail of smells to tell other ants where food can be found.

▶ Baby birds make sounds to tell their parents they are hungry.

1. What does *communicate* mean?
   a. share information
   b. leave a trail of smells
   c. do a special dance

2. Explain two ways that animals *communicate* that you learned about in the passage.

   _____

   _____

3. What is a way that you can *communicate* without talking?

   _____

   _____

   _____

Name: _____

How Animals Share Information

Animals use different senses when they share information. When a cat rubs up against your leg, it is **sharing information**. It is communicating. What do you think the cat could be trying to tell you?

Some animals communicate with *sound*:

- The wolves in a pack howl to one another.
- Birds chirp and sing.
- Frogs hear one another croak.
- Humans can communicate by talking.

Smell is important in many animals' communication:

- Snakes pick up smells with their tongues.
- Wolves, deer, and elephants make smells so their families can find them. Fish and ants can put out a smell that tells others that danger is near.

Wolf howling

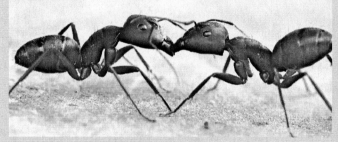

Ants communicating with touch

Some animals share information through *touch*:

- Elephant mothers touch their babies with their trunks to calm them.
- Ants touch their antennae together. This sends messages.

---

1. What is another way to say *share information*?
    a. eat together   **b.** communicate   **c.** trade games

2. Explain two ways that animals communicate that you read about in the passage.

_____

_____

_____

3. Write about one way that you communicate with your friends or family.

_____

_____

_____

Name: _____

Can Plants Communicate?

Have you ever smelled grass right after it was cut? Most people love the smell of cut grass. It turns out that the smell is important. It's grass calling for help!

Plants can't talk, or even make noise. So, how do they communicate? They share information by releasing **chemicals**. Each chemical a plant releases means something different, the way each word means something different.

Plants can release different chemicals together, such as putting words together to make a sentence. Some chemical sentences say "Help!" to nearby plants. Others say, "Stay away!" to bugs.

These **chemical messages** can go through the air. The plants' leaves put them out and take them in. Messages can also be sent and received through roots in the soil.

When a bug chews the leaves of a poplar tree, the tree releases chemicals into the air. The other poplar trees nearby detect it. They start putting out different chemicals that will keep the bugs away.

Plants can even communicate with bugs. When a bug called a cutworm attacks corn, the corn plant sends out clouds of chemicals. These chemicals cause wasps to come and lay their eggs in the cutworms. This kills the cutworms and helps the corn plant.

1. How do plants communicate? _____

_____

2. What are two ways that *chemical messages* travel? _____

_____

3. Why do corn plants put out chemicals that attract wasps?
   a. so the wasps will kill cutworms on the corn
   b. so the wasps will lay their eggs on the corn
   c. so the cutworms will leave the corn alone

Name: _____

Animal Life Cycles

An animal's **life cycle** is the story of its life. It has a beginning, a middle, and an end.

First, an animal is **born**. Then, it **grows** into an adult. Adult animals can **reproduce**. That means they make baby animals like themselves. Finally, all animals **die**.

Different kinds of animals have different life cycles. Some animals are born alive. Other animals hatch from eggs. Some baby animals look like their parents. Other baby animals look very different from their parents. They change as they grow up.

All animals can reproduce. They have baby animals that will grow up to be just like them. No animal can live forever. Someday, they must die. Their babies will live on. They will grow up and reproduce. Their life cycles will keep going.

1. Which choice shows the stages of an animal *life cycle* in the right order?
   a. birth, growth, reproduction, death
   b. growth, birth, death, reproduction
   c. birth, reproduction, growth, death

2. What are two ways baby animals can be born?

   _____

   _____

   _____

3. What do you think would happen if animals stopped *reproducing*?

   _____

   _____

   _____

Name: _____

Animals: Birth and Growth

Animals are **born** in different ways. Some animals come from eggs. Chickens lay eggs. Their baby chicks **hatch** out of the eggs. Other animals grow inside their mother until they are born. Baby elephants grow inside mother elephants. They are born alive.

Some young animals look like their parents when they are born. When baby alligators hatch, they look like tiny adult alligators. A new puppy has the same kind of body as an adult dog, but it is smaller. Even baby humans, like you, have the same body parts as adults. When we grow up, we keep the same body parts. Our bodies just get bigger.

Other animals look very different from their parents when they are born. A baby frog is called a tadpole. It looks more like a fish. It lives in the water and has a tail. It does not have legs like an adult frog. A baby butterfly is a caterpillar. It looks very different from an adult butterfly. These animals change as they grow. When they become adults, they look like their parents.

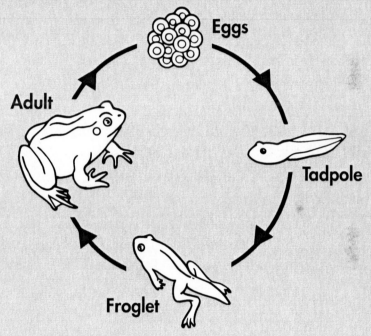

1. What is the main idea of this passage?
    a. Some animals have babies.
    b. Some baby animals look like their parents, and some do not.
    c. Some animals come from eggs.

2. Name three animal babies that look like their parents.

    _____ _____ _____

3. Describe how you have changed since you were born.

    _____

    _____

    _____

Name: _____

Mammal Life Cycles

Mammals are a kind of animal. Mammals give birth to live babies. Mammal mothers feed their babies with milk from their bodies.

When mammal babies are born, they have the same kind of bodies as their parents. Baby lions look like little adult lions. Puppies look like small versions of adult dogs. Humans are mammals, too. When you were born, you had the same kind of body as your parents, but smaller.

Baby mammals drink milk from their mothers. This means they must stay with their mothers after they are born. As they grow up, they learn to eat food like their parents.

Baby mammals grow into adult mammals. They live, they reproduce (have babies), and they die. Some mammals have short life cycles. Mice usually live for just one year. Some mammals live for a very long time. Blue whales can live to be 110 years old!

1. Write two facts about *mammals* from the passage.

   Fact 1: _____

   Fact 2: _____

2. Draw a line from each text box to the correct picture.

1 1-year-old feeding self	2 adult with own family	3 baby giraffe drinking milk	4 young adult 6 years old

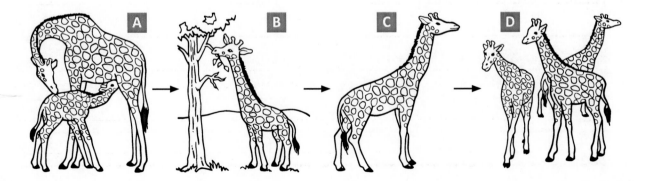

Name: _____

Reptile and Amphibian Life Cycles

Reptiles and amphibians are both **cold-blooded**. This means they need sunlight to warm themselves up. Reptiles and amphibians have different life cycles.

Snakes, turtles, and lizards are **reptiles.** Most reptiles, such as crocodiles and tortoises, lay eggs. The eggs have soft shells. The babies have an egg tooth to rip their way out of the eggs.

Sea turtles

Other reptiles, like some kinds of snakes, give birth to live babies. Reptile babies look just like their parents. As they grow, they just get bigger. The shapes of their bodies don't change much.

Tadpole with tail and legs

Frogs, toads, and salamanders are **amphibians**. Amphibians lay eggs in water. When the eggs hatch, the babies live in water. Amphibian babies do not look like their parents! They have gills to breathe and tails to swim. As they get older, they grow legs. They lose their tails. Some grow lungs and begin to breathe air. After they grow up, they look like their parents.

1. How do *cold-blooded* animals warm up?

_____

_____

2. Complete this graphic organizer about *reptiles* and *amphibians*. Write one or two facts from the passage in each section.

Amphibians	Reptiles
_____	_____
_____	_____
_____	_____

B o t h	_____
	_____

Name: _____

Insect Life Cycles

There are two kinds of insect life cycles. One has three stages and one has four stages.

Three Stages

Insects such as dragonflies have three life stages: **egg**, **nymph**, and **adult**.

Dragonflies lay eggs on water plants in a pond. Nymphs hatch from the eggs. They live in the water. Dragonfly nymphs do not look like adult dragonflies.

A nymph wears its skeleton on the outside, like a shell. It is called an **exoskeleton.** A nymph has to **molt** to grow. This means the old exoskeleton breaks apart. Then, it crawls out of it.

Each time a nymph molts, it changes a little. Dragonfly nymphs can molt up to 15 times before they become adults!

1. Label the dragonfly life cycle diagram.

Word Bank
adult
egg
nymph

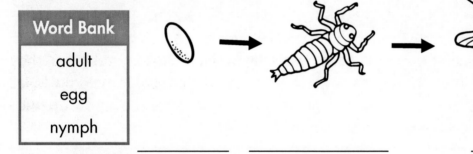

_____   _____   _____

Four Stages

Insects such as butterflies have four life stages: **egg**, **larva**, **pupa**, and **adult**.

Larvae hatch from eggs. Butterfly **larvae** are called caterpillars. They do not look like adult butterflies. They eat a lot and grow quickly.

The larva makes a hard outer shell around itself. This is the **pupa** stage. It stays inside the shell while its body changes. When it comes out, it is an adult.

2. Label the butterfly life cycle diagram.

Word Bank
adult
egg
larva
pupa

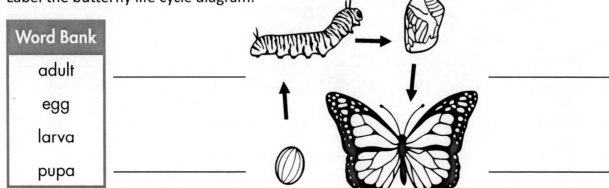

Name: _____

Inherited Traits

When a cat has babies, why don't they look like dogs? Or hamsters? Why are the **offspring** of cats always kittens and not other animals?

All plants and animals **inherit** traits from their parents. **Traits** are passed from parents to their offspring. These traits decide what plants and animals look like. Cat parents pass on their traits to their kittens. This is why kittens look like small cats and not like puppies or hamsters or elephants.

It works the same way for plants. What do apple seeds grow into? Not broccoli or cactus! Apple trees grow from apple seeds. Young apple trees grow to look like their parents. They have the same traits.

What kinds of traits do animal parents pass on to their young? Things such as the size and shape of the body, the number of legs, the kind of skin covering, and the shapes of teeth. In plants, inherited traits can include the plant's height, the shape of the leaves, the color of flowers, and the kind of fruit and seeds produced.

1. What does *inherit* mean?
   a. get from parents   **b.** the size of a leaf   **c.** reproduce

2. Name two *traits* that can be inherited in animals.

   Animals

   Trait 1: _____   **Trait 2:** _____

3. Name two *traits* that can be inherited in plants.

   Plants

   Trait 1: _____   **Trait 2:** _____

4. What are two *traits* that you have inherited from your parents?

   Trait 1: _____   **Trait 2:** _____

Name: _____

Traits Change Over Time

Do all kittens look exactly like their cat parents? No!

Some kitten traits come from the mother. Some traits come from the father. A kitten might have the same color eyes as its mother but the same color fur as its father. So, the kittens look like their parents, but not exactly the same.

The same is true for people. You get some traits from your mother and some traits from your father. These **traits** decide how you look. Nobody in the world, not even your sister or brother, has the exact same traits as you.

People do this with plants, too. If you put together plants that have big tomatoes, some of the **offspring** of those plants will have even bigger tomatoes. If you do this enough times, you will have a plant that grows very big tomatoes!

1. Which of these is not an example of a *trait*?
   a. hair color
   b. eye color
   c. shirt color

2. What is the main idea of this passage?
   a. People are trying to grow bigger and bigger tomatoes.
   b. Living things look like, but not exactly like, their parents.
   c. You have a brother or a sister.

3. Why do brothers and sisters look alike, but not exactly alike?

   _____

   _____

   _____

   _____

Name: _____

Acquired Traits

Not all the traits of living things come from their parents. Some traits happen during a plant or animal's life. These are called **acquired traits**.

Anything an animal learns is an acquired trait.

- Himalayan rabbits have white fur. If the temperature gets cold enough, the fur on their ears, nose, feet, and tail will turn black. Black fur helps keep these body parts warm. The black fur is an acquired trait caused by the temperature.

- Dogs can learn commands, such as "sit" and "stay."

- Cats can learn to use a litter box.

Plants can also acquire traits.

- Some plants need a lot of sunlight to grow. If they are planted in a shady place, they will not grow as big.

- People cut plants into different shapes. Their shapes are acquired traits.

Humans can acquire traits, too.

- Things people do can change the way they look. If they don't eat enough, they will become very thin. If they eat a lot, they can get heavier.

- Playing sports or lifting weights can change the shape of people's bodies.

- Do you have any scars? They are acquired. They will not be passed on to your children.

- Some people can get freckles if they go out in the sunlight. If they don't go out in the sunlight, the freckles don't show up!

- You are not born knowing a language. You learn to speak from the people around you.

Some traits can be both inherited and acquired. You inherit the color of your skin, but spending time in sunlight can make skin darker. Things you learn, such as how to read or play an instrument, are acquired traits. Talent for playing a musical instrument can be inherited, but you won't get good unless you practice!

1. What does *acquire* mean?
   a. to get   **b.** to lose   **c.** to inherit

2. How can living things *acquire traits*?
   a. learn them   **b.** get them as you grow   **c.** both

3. What are some traits that you have acquired?

_____

Name: _____

Inherited or Acquired?

Directions: Write each human trait in the correct place in the Venn diagram.

Traits

- ☐ eye color
- ☐ eating with a fork
- ☐ scars
- ☐ hair color
- ☐ size of ears
- ☐ skin color
- ☐ language spoken
- ☐ playing piano

Venn Diagram

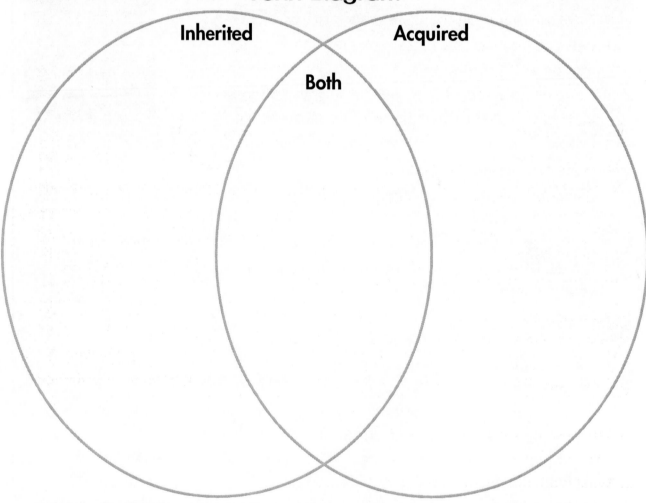

Inherited   **Acquired**

Both

Inherited traits are traits you are born with. You get them from your parents.

Acquired traits are traits you get or learn as you grow up.

Name: _____

The Best of Its Kind

An animal's **traits** help it survive. A giraffe's long neck is a trait. It helps the giraffe reach food up high in trees. Different traits help animals **survive**. That means that they can stay alive. Different traits can also help an animal **reproduce**. When an animal reproduces, it has babies. These babies are called **offspring**.

The Best Tools

Hummingbirds drink nectar from flowers. Sometimes, a hummingbird's beak is a better shape for reaching into flowers than other hummingbirds' beaks. This bird will get more food. This makes it more likely to survive and have offspring.

The Best Camouflage

If a mouse's fur is the color of the ground where it lives, it will be hard for predators to see it. This mouse can hide better. Its fur is a kind of camouflage. Mice with fur that does not match the ground have a problem. They are more likely to be seen and eaten by predators.

So, the mouse with the best camouflage has a better chance to survive and reproduce.

The Best Colors

Male peacocks have very large, colorful tails. They fan out their tails to attract females. Sometimes, a male peacock has a bigger, more colorful tail than the other nearby males. The females will choose him. He is more likely to reproduce.

The traits that help an animal survive and reproduce can be passed on to its offspring.

1. What does the word *survive* mean?
   a. to eat   **b.** to live   **c.** to reproduce

2. What is another word for *offspring*?
   a. reproduce   **b.** babies   **c.** camouflage

3. Why is it important for animals to *reproduce*?
   a. so they can find places to hide   **c.** to make more animals like themselves
   b. so they can find food

4. How could you camouflage yourself in the forest?

_____

_____

Name: _____

What Are Biomes?

Not all of Earth is the same. Some places get a lot of rain. Some places don't get very much rain at all. Some places are hot, some are cold, and some can be both. Scientists call these different kinds of places **biomes**. Biomes are very large areas of Earth.

Here are some different biomes:

Desert biomes get very little rain. They are usually sunny because there are no clouds. Not all deserts are hot. There are some very cold deserts! The plants in a desert don't need a lot of water.

Forest biomes have a lot of trees. They get a lot of rain or snow, which helps the trees grow. The tall trees block the Sun, so the forest floor is shady.

Grassland biomes get enough rain for grasses to grow, but not enough for a lot of trees. They get a lot of sun and wind. Grasslands are usually located between deserts and forests.

Tundra biomes are the coldest biome. They get little or no rain, and there are no trees. Tundra lands are frozen most of the time. In the summer, the top few inches of the ground thaw out. The soil is shallow, wet, and squishy. Sometimes flowers bloom.

The **aquatic** biome has two **regions**: freshwater and marine.

- The **freshwater regions** include ponds and lakes, streams and rivers, and wetlands.
- The **marine region** includes the oceans, where the water is salty.

1. The *desert* and *tundra* are alike because they both _____.
      a. are cold biomes.   **b.** get very little rain.   **c.** have a lot of trees.

2. What *biome* is usually located between forests and deserts? _____

3. What is the main difference between the two regions of the *aquatic* biome?

_____

_____

Desert, Greg Rakozy on Unsplash. Forest, Jesse Gardner on Unsplash. Grassland, Stefan Strebl on Unsplash.

26   *#8263 Let's Get This Day Started: Science*   ©*Teacher Created Resources*

Name: _____

Nonliving Parts of Biomes

Biomes have both living and nonliving parts. The living parts are the plants and animals. These are some of the nonliving parts:

Sunlight

Sunlight is the main source of energy on Earth. Each biome gets different amounts of sunlight. The amount of sunlight in a biome can change depending on the time of year.

Temperature

A biome can be hot during the day and cold at night, or hot in the summer and cold in the winter. Some places, such as rainforests, can be warm all the time.

Water

All living things need water to survive. Some places, such as oceans and ponds, have a lot of water. Other places, such as deserts, have very little water. The amount of water that falls as rain or snow in an area can change with the seasons.

Soil

Soil, sand, gravel, and dirt are made from broken-down rocks. Soil can also have some **decomposed** plants and animals. Soils are different in different biomes. Soil can be dry and sandy in deserts. Soil can be moist and full of decomposed living material in forests.

1. What is the main source of energy on Earth?
   a. sunlight   **b.** temperature   **c.** soil

2. What are *decomposed* plants and animals?
   a. young plants and animals that reproduce
   b. plants and animals that do not like much sunlight
   c. dead plants and animals that are turning back into soil

3. Choose one biome and describe its nonliving parts.

Biome	desert	forest	grassland	tundra	aquatic

Biome: _____

Sunlight: _____

Temperature: _____

Water: _____

Soil: _____

Name: _____

Interpreting Graphs: Biomes

Directions: Use the data tables for **Site A** and **Site B** to answer the questions below.

Site A		
Month	**Average Temperature (°F)**	**Average Rainfall**
January	75°	0
April	82°	0
July	110°	1 inch
October	96°	1 inch

1. What is the highest temperature for **Site A**? _____

   What is the lowest temperature for **Site A**? _____

   What is the difference between the highest and the lowest temperature? _____

2. What is the most rainfall that **Site A** gets in a month? _____

3. What biome is **Site A** in? _____

   Why? _____

Site B		
Month	**Average Temperature (°F)**	**Average Rainfall**
January	85°	8 inches
April	80°	8 inches
July	82°	7 inches
October	81°	7 inches

4. What is the highest temperature for **Site B**? _____

   What is the lowest temperature for **Site B**? _____

   What is the difference between the highest and the lowest temperature? _____

5. What can you tell about the rainfall that **Site B** gets? _____

6. What biome is **Site B** in? _____

   Why? _____

Name: _____

Biome Plants

Directions: Read about each plant. Then, name the biome where you think it lives.

Biomes	aquatic	desert	forest	grassland	tundra

1. Buffalo Grass

This short grass grows quickly and covers a large area. It needs plenty of sunlight.

Biome: _____

2. Saguaro Cactus

This very tall cactus plant is adapted to go without water for a long time. It can absorb a lot of water when it rains. Then it uses the water slowly over a long time when there is no rain.

Biome: _____

3. Eastern White Pine

This tall tree has leaves shaped like needles. The needles absorb sunlight. These trees usually grow close to one another and create shade on the ground.

Biome: _____

4. Caribou Moss

This small plant grows very low to the ground. It can survive a long time without light or water. Very cold temperatures do not damage this moss.

Biome: _____

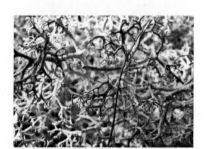

5. Kelp

Kelp plants have a root-like base called a *holdfast* that helps them stick to the ocean floor. They have air-filled balloons on their leaves that help them float up toward the sunlight.

Biome: _____

Name: _____

Ecosystems

Each biome has different ecosystems in it. An **ecosystem** includes all the living and nonliving things in an area.

Here are two different kinds of ecosystems in the **forest** biome:

Rainforests

Rainforests get lots and lots of rain. The temperature is warm all the time. More kinds of plants and animals live in rainforest ecosystems than in any other ecosystems in the world. Animals such as toucans and sloths live in rainforests. Most rainforests are found along the equator. This means they get lots of sunlight all year long.

Deciduous Forests

Deciduous forests have warm summers and cold winters with lots of snow. **Deciduous** means the tree leaves fall off in the winter. The leaves grow back in the spring when it gets warmer. Deer, squirrels, and woodpeckers live in these forests.

1. Black bears eat a lot of food over the summer and fall. They get very fat. During the winter, they hibernate. They go into their dens and sleep until it gets warmer in the spring.

   Are black bears more likely to live in a rainforest or a deciduous forest?

   Rainforest   Deciduous Forest

   Why? _____

   _____

2. Boa constrictors are large snakes. They live in trees. They are **cold-blooded** animals, which means they cannot make their own heat.

   Are boa constrictors more likely to live in a rainforest or a deciduous forest?

   Rainforest   Deciduous Forest

   Why? _____

   _____

Name: _____

Physical Adaptations to Get Food

A **habitat** is a place where an animal lives. **Physical adaptations** are body parts that help animals survive in their habitats. Different body parts help animals get food, run fast, and protect themselves. Long necks, talons, and sharp teeth are all physical adaptations.

A bird's beak is another example of a physical adaptation. Different kinds of beaks can get different kinds of food.

Spoonbills are large birds. Spoonbill beaks look like flat spoons! These birds swish their beaks from side to side in the water as they walk. They scoop up prey with their spoon beaks.

Crossbills are small birds. Their beaks are crossed at the tip. (Look closely at the tip of the crossbill's beak in the picture.) These unusual beaks help crossbills pull seeds out of closed pinecones.

1. What is an example of a *physical adaptation*?
   a. looking for food to eat
   b. a place where an animal lives
   c. body parts that help animals survive

2. What kind of *habitat* do spoonbills live in? What is your evidence?

   Water   They use their beaks

3. What kind of *habitat* do crossbills live in? What is your evidence?

   crossbills live in the forest

4. Do you think a spoonbill could survive in the crossbill's *habitat*? Why, or why not?

   The forest hee's to be near water

Name: _____

Physical Adaptations for Protection

Some *physical adaptations* are body parts that help animals protect themselves from **predators**.

- Some adaptations help animals hide from predators.
- Other adaptations can scare predators away.

Snowshoe hares look like big rabbits. They eat flowers and grasses. They have two physical adaptations that help keep them safe from predators. First, they can run very fast. Second, they use **camouflage**. This means their bodies can blend in with their habitat. That makes it hard for predators to see them.

In the summer, snowshoe hares' fur is brown. It looks like the dirt and rocks. In the winter, their fur turns white like the snow.

Porcupines live in forests. They move slowly and do not see very well. They spend a lot of their time in the trees. They eat leaves, twigs, bark, and berries. They have sharp quills all over their bodies to protect them.

1. What is a *predator*?
   a. a kind of camouflage
   b. an animal that eats other animals
   c. a kind of snake

2. How does a snowshoe hare's fur keep it safe?
   a. It is hard for predators to see the hare.
   b. It is hard for predators to smell the hare.
   c. It is hard for predators to hear the hare.

3. What is another *physical adaptation* that helps keep snowshoe hares safe?

   _____

   _____

4. What *physical adaptation* of porcupines protects them from predators?
   a. They spend a lot of time in trees.
   b. They have sharp quills all over their bodies.
   c. They eat twigs and bark that other animals want.

Name: _____

Physical Adaptations to Stay Warm or Cool

Some **physical adaptations** help animals stay cool when the weather is hot. Other adaptations keep them warm when it is cold.

Hot Habitats

Many animals live in hot habitats. They have body parts to help them keep cool. Fennec foxes and jackrabbits have very large ears that give off body heat.

Ostriches do not have feathers on their heads, necks, legs, and feet. In the summer, their bare skin gives off heat to keep them cool. When it is cold in the winter, they can fold their wings over their legs to keep warm.

Cold Habitats

Animals that live in cold habitats have body parts to keep them warm. Polar bears may look white, but their fur has no color. Their skin is black. The Sun shines through their fur and heats the dark skin underneath. This keeps them warm.

Polar bears, whales, and seals also have a thick layer of fat called **blubber**. The blubber helps keep them warm, even in freezing water.

1. Which statement is true?
    a. Ostriches have large ears.
    b. Fennec foxes have bare skin on their legs.
    c. Polar bears have black skin.

2. How does a seal's body help it stay warm in freezing waters?

   _____

   _____

3. Name a *physical adaptation* for each animal.

   fox _____

   ostrich _____

   polar bear _____

Fennec fox, Eric Johnston, CC BY-SA 3.0.

Physical Adaptations of Plants

Plants have **physical adaptations** to help them live and grow. They are adapted to one kind of habitat. They cannot survive in places where they cannot get what they need.

Some plant parts help a plant get what it needs to grow. Their leaves absorb sunlight and convert it to energy. Their roots take up water and nutrients from the soil.

Thorns

Plants can have parts that protect them from being eaten. Some plants have thorns or spines. Others have fruits or leaves that taste bad. Nuts can be hard for an animal to break open.

Plant parts can help a plant survive in harsh weather. Some plants can grow even in the Arctic cold. They grow low to the ground and have fuzzy stems and leaves to keep them warm. Some plants can grow in hot, dry habitats. They have few leaves. They can store water in their thick stems.

1. How can thorns help a plant survive?
   a. Thorns help the plant get water.
   b. Thorns help protect the plant from being eaten.
   c. Thorns help the plant survive in harsh weather.

2. Name two parts of a plant that help it get what it needs to grow.

   _____

   _____

3. Do you think a cactus could live in the Arctic?   **Yes**   **No**

   Why or why not? _____

   _____

   _____

   _____

Name: _Lily Grunauer_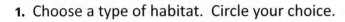
2/7/22

Invent an Animal

1. Choose a type of habitat. Circle your choice.

| arctic | dry desert | pine forest | grassland | pond | ocean |

2. List some physical adaptations that an animal would need to survive in that habitat.

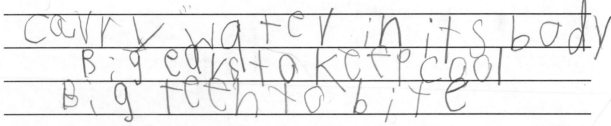

carry water in its body
Big ears to keep cool
Big teeth to bite

3. Invent a new animal that is adapted to your habitat. Describe your animal and how it is adapted to its habitat.

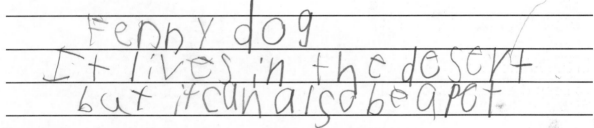

Fenny dog
It lives in the desert
but it can also be a pet

4. Draw your new animal in its habitat. Label its physical adaptations.

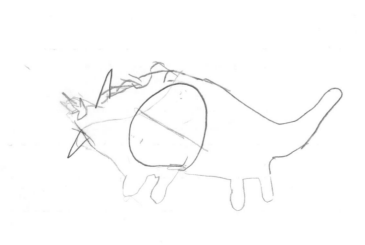

Name: _____

Instincts for Getting Food

There are some things an animal just knows how to do. No one has to teach them. They are called **instincts**. Some instincts help animals get food.

- A spider makes a web to catch food. No one teaches the spider how to spin a web. It just knows. Making a web is an instinct.

- Squirrels know how to hide food. When the weather is warm, they gather nuts and hide them. In the winter, they can find them again.

- Crocodiles hold very still. They wait for prey to come near. Then, they lunge toward the prey and grab it with their powerful jaws.

- Tigers stalk their **prey**. They get down low. They move very slowly and carefully. The prey does not see them coming. When they get close, they jump! Tigers know how to stalk their prey to get food, even when they are very young.

1. Which animal surprises its *prey*?
   a. tiger
   b. spider
   c. squirrel

2. Why do you think squirrels need to hide food?

   _____

   _____

3. What is an *instinct*?

   _____

   _____

Name: _____

Learned Behaviors for Getting Food

Sometimes, animals' instincts are not enough to help them get food. They must **learn** to find food in their habitats.

Scientists studied birds called mountain chickadees. Some chickadees lived high up on the mountain where there was a lot of snow. Another group of chickadees lived lower down the mountain. Lower down, the winters weren't quite as bad.

The scientists tested the birds. They put out special containers of bird food. The birds had to figure out how to open the containers. Then, they could get the food. The scientists also watched the birds hide some of their food. They wanted to see if the birds remembered where they hid the food.

Scientists discovered that the chickadees that lived higher up the mountain were smarter. They could figure out how to open food containers faster. The birds remembered where they hid their food. They also remembered where the hiding places were for a longer time.

Scientists think this is because the birds that lived higher up on the mountain needed to be smarter to survive. It was harder for them to find food because of the snow. The birds learned better ways to find food in their habitat.

1. What did the scientists do?
   a. They opened containers of food.
   b. They hid food for the birds.
   c. They observed the chickadees.

2. What do you think might happen to the chickadees higher up the mountain if they did not *learn* better ways to find food in their habitat?

   _____

   _____

3. What are some things you have learned how to do?

   _____

   _____

   _____

Name: _____

Behaviors to Stay Safe

Animals act in different ways to protect themselves. These actions are called **behaviors**. Some behaviors keep animals safe from predators.

➡ Hiding is a behavior. Many animals hide from predators. Clown fish hide in the stinging tentacles of sea anemones. They don't feel the stinging. Other fish can hide in the sand at the bottom of the ocean. They lie down and wiggle around until the sand covers them up.

➡ Some animals stay very still to fool predators. They "freeze." When an opossum sees a predator, it lies down and pretends to be dead. Then, the predator leaves it alone. Rabbits stay very still when they know a predator is near. The predator might not see them if they don't move.

➡ Some animals help one another. When a prairie dog sees a predator, it makes a sound. The sound tells the other prairie dogs that danger is near. The sound tells what kind of predator it is. They have different sounds for hawks, snakes, and coyotes.

1. What is the main idea of this passage?
   a. Some behaviors keep animals safe from predators.
   b. Some animals make special sounds to help one other.
   c. Many animals know how to hide from predators.

2. What *behavior* do opossums use to keep safe from predators?
   a. They run away.
   b. They play dead.
   c. They make a sound.

3. Prairie dogs make _____ to warn others of danger.

4. What *behaviors* do you use to stay safe?

   _____

   _____

Name: _____

Behaviors to Stay Warm or Cool

Some **behaviors** help animals survive when it gets very cold or very hot.

- Many animals **migrate**. They move from one place to another to stay warm and to find food. Whales and birds both migrate very long distances. This is a **behavioral adaptation**. It is something the animals do to survive in their habitats.

- Some animals **hibernate**. When winter comes, they go into a protected place. They sleep while it is cold outside. In the spring, when it is warmer, they wake up. Then, they can find food.

- Emperor penguins **huddle** together to survive Arctic winter storms. Thousands of penguins form a tightly packed group. They share the warmth of their bodies.

- In some habitats, it gets very hot in the daytime. Some animals hide and sleep in the hot part of the day. Some smaller animals burrow under the ground where it is cooler. They come out to look for food at night when it cools down.

- Elephants use their trunks to blow dirt all over themselves. Rhinos roll in the mud. The mud and dirt protect the animals' skin. They keep them cool in the hot sunlight.

1. What does *migrate* mean?
   a. roll around in the mud
   b. go to sleep when it is cold
   c. move from one place to another

2. Why do some animals *hibernate* in the winter?

   _____

   _____

3. What do you do to stay warm when it is cold outside?

   _____

   _____

   _____

Name: _____

Behaviors in Plants

Scientists disagree on whether plants can have behaviors. Plants cannot think or make decisions. But they can move! They just move much slower than most animals.

The stems and leaves of plants grow toward the Sun. Roots always grow down, no matter which way the plant is turned.

Some plants can move their leaves and flowers. Some flowers open in the daytime and close each night. Other flowers only open at night. Some plants move their leaves to follow the movement of the Sun over a day.

A few plants can move quickly. A Venus flytrap can close on an insect. It uses the insect for food. A mimosa plant folds in its leaves quickly if it is touched.

Venus flytrap

What do you think—do plants have behaviors? Explain your thinking.

_____

_____

_____

_____

_____

_____

_____

Name: _____

When Habitats Change

A **habitat** is a place that has everything an animal needs to survive. Sometimes habitats change. Habitats can change quickly or slowly. There are many causes of habitat change.

Sometimes, people change a habitat. They cut down trees to make room for farms. They build roads and towns where there used to be grasslands. Pollution can get into the air or into lakes, streams, or oceans.

Habitats can change naturally, too. Fires can burn large areas of forests or grasslands. Too much rain or melting snow can cause floods. Not enough rain can cause drought. Big storms can damage habitats.

When a plant or an animal's habitat changes, they might not be able to get what they need to survive. Some can **adapt**, or change, and survive. Raccoons, coyotes, and crows have learned to live in cities. They can find food and shelter there.

Crow

Some plants and animals move to a new place that has what they need. Some living things die when their habitat changes. They cannot adapt or move to a new place. Many kinds of plants and animals are **threatened**, or **endangered**, because their habitats have changed. This means there are not many of them left.

1. Which statement is true?
   a. Some animals can adapt when their habitat changes.
   b. All animals can move to a new place when their habitat changes.
   c. Some animals can cause floods.

2. Name three ways that a *habitat* can change.

   _____   _____   _____

3. What can happen to plants and animals when their *habitat* changes?

   _____

   _____

   _____

Name: _____

Raccoons and Habitat Change

Sometimes, the place where an animal lives, its habitat, can change. Some animals can **adapt** to the changed habitat. They can learn to get what they need.

Raccoons usually live in the forest. They eat bugs, frogs, fish, eggs, nuts, seeds, and fruits. They find their food in their habitat.

Sometimes, people build homes and cities where raccoons live. The food that the raccoons usually eat is gone. What can the forest raccoons do? They could leave and look for another place that has the food they are used to. But most of the time, raccoons stay. They learn to find and eat new kinds of food.

City raccoons are very good at getting things open. They can open trash cans, chip bags, and all sorts of containers that have food inside.

When scientists observed city raccoons and forest raccoons, they found that the city raccoons are smarter. They are also less afraid of new things. They adapted to their changed habitat.

1. What does the word *adapt* mean?
   a. leave   **b.** change   **c.** stay

2. What is the main idea of this passage?
   a. Raccoons can open trash cans.
   b. Raccoons are smart.
   c. Raccoons can adapt to changes in their habitat.

3. What animals have you seen where you live?

   _____   _____   _____

   How do you think these animals *adapted* to living near people?

   _____

   _____

   _____

   _____

Name: _____

Save the Ferrets!

Sometimes, an animal's **habitat** changes. Some animals can't adapt to changes in their habitats. They can't get what they need anymore.

Black-footed ferrets live in grasslands. Their habitats are called **prairies**. They eat prairie dogs, so they live where the prairie dogs live. Ferrets need to catch a lot of prairie dogs to eat. One ferret can eat more than 100 prairie dogs in a year! Ferrets live and nest in old prairie-dog burrows.

Black-footed ferret

What happens when people build farms or cities on the land where the prairie dogs and ferrets live?

Prairie dogs need the plants in the grasslands to eat. Farmers try to get rid of prairie dogs. They do not want the prairie dogs digging on their farms. They don't want them eating the plants.

Prairie dogs cannot live in the new cities. They cannot find enough plants to eat. They cannot find places to make homes.

Ferrets die if they cannot find enough prairie dogs to eat. Black-footed ferrets are **endangered**. This means there are not many of them left. When people changed the ferret habitat, the animals could not adapt. They could not survive.

At one time, there were only 18 black-footed ferrets left! People wanted to help. Some zoos took ferrets to keep them safe. In the zoos, the ferrets got food and had babies. They were safe.

People also worked to bring back prairies. They helped some ferrets go back to the prairies. Now, there are 300 black-footed ferrets in zoos and about 1,000 in the wild.

1. What does it mean when a kind of animal or plant is *endangered*?
   a. There aren't many left.   **b.** They live in a habitat.   **c.** They need a lot to eat.

2. What do animals need to survive?

   _____

3. Why are black-footed ferrets *endangered*?

   _____

   _____

Name: _____

Help the Warblers!

The golden-cheeked warbler is a small bird. It lives in Texas. These warblers only nest in trees called Ashe junipers. They find their food in these trees. The birds eat the insects they find. They use spider webs and the bark of Ashe junipers to build their nests. The Ashe juniper is where the warbler lives and eats!

Sometimes, people do things that cause harm to an animal species. They build roads, homes, and farms on animal habitats. People in Texas have cut down many Ashe juniper trees for wood and also to build roads, farms, and homes. What happens when Ashe junipers are cut down? The golden-cheeked warblers cannot find food. They cannot nest. They cannot raise babies. That is why these birds are endangered.

Golden-cheeked warbler

But people can also help fix things! They can **restore** habitats. This means they can work to make a place the way it was before. This helps endangered animals and plants. People are working to restore the habitat for the little birds. They are planting new Ashe juniper trees.

1. Why does the golden-cheeked warbler need the Ashe juniper tree?
   a. for food
   b. for bark to build their nests
   c. both **a** and **b**

2. What does it mean to *restore* a habitat?
   a. Make it bigger than it was.
   b. Make it the way it was.
   c. Make it better than it was.

3. What are people doing to help the warblers?

   _____

   _____

   _____

Name: _____

Natural or Manmade Change?

Habitats can change quickly or slowly. There are many causes of habitat change. Sometimes, people change a habitat. That is called **manmade change**. Habitat change can also be **natural**, or not caused by people.

Directions: Read each description of habitat change, and circle **Manmade** or **Natural**.

1	A very big hurricane moves over land. Many trees are knocked down. A lot of the land is flooded.

                Natural   **Manmade**

2	A big ship has an accident. Oil spills into the ocean. The oil stays in the water and on the shore for many years.

                Natural   **Manmade**

3	Lightning strikes a grassland. A fire starts. It spreads quickly.

                Natural   **Manmade**

4	A beaver cuts down trees and builds a dam. Some forestland is flooded. A pond is formed.

                Natural   **Manmade**

5	Many acres of rainforest are cut down. Farm crops are planted in their place.

                Natural   **Manmade**

6	Water is pumped out of a river. It is sent to homes, schools, and stores. The river has a lot less water in it.

                Natural   **Manmade**

Name: _____

What Is a Fossil?

Fossils are what are left of plants and animals that lived long ago. These remains are found all over the world. There are two main kinds of fossils:

Body fossils are the hard parts of a plant or an animal. Bones and teeth can become body fossils. Plant stems and branches can also become body fossils.

Body fossils, such as those of dinosaurs, can be very large. Some animal fossils can be so small that you need a microscope to see them!

Most of the fossils found on Earth are body fossils.

Trace fossils tell us about how animals lived in the past. Trace fossils include things such as footprints and poop!

➡ Footprints can tell us about how animals moved and acted.

➡ Fossil poop can tell us a lot about what animals ate.

1. What is a *fossil*?
   a. a rock that has been around for years
   b. the remains of a plant or an animal
   c. a one-celled animal

2. What are the two kinds of fossils?

   _____

   _____

   _____

3. What do you already know about fossils and things that lived long ago?

   _____

   _____

   _____

   _____

   _____

Name: _____

How Do Fossils Form?

Living things **decay** when they die. They break into tiny bits and become part of the dirt. Most things decay completely. But sometimes, the hard parts of animals, such as bones and teeth, become fossils.

If an animal dies in the right place, **sediment** buries its skeleton. Sediment is dirt, sand, or mud. A dead animal must be buried quickly to become a fossil. Many fossils are formed when dead animals sink to the bottom of an ocean or a muddy place.

Over millions of years, layers of sediment build up. The layers push down on one another. This **pressure** turns the layers to rock. Inside the rock, the bones of the dead animal dissolve. They break into tiny pieces and go into the water. **Minerals** in the water replace the bones. That is a fossil! A fossil is made of rock, not bone.

Earth is always changing. Over millions of years, the layer of rock that holds a fossil can rise to the surface. What used to be an ocean might now be a desert. The rock wears away in the rain and wind. The fossil is **exposed**. It can be seen.

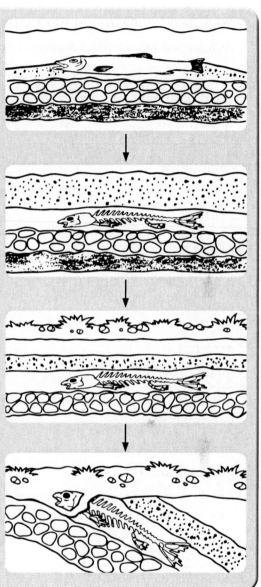

1. What does the word *decay* mean?

_____

_____

2. What are fossils made of?
   a. bone   **b.** rock   **c.** sediment

3. Do you think a jellyfish could become a body fossil? Why, or why not?

_____

_____

Name: _____

What Can Fossils Tell Us?

Fossils give us clues about the past. Fossils are formed in layers of sedimentary rock. The bottom layer of rock is the oldest. The top layer of rock is the newest. Fossils found in the same layer of rock probably lived at the same time.

If plant fossils are found, that tells more about what the land was like at that time.

Scientists can tell a lot about an animal from a fossil:

- They can tell how big it was from the size of the bones or shells.
- The teeth of an animal show what kind of food it probably ate.
- The size of the skull can tell how big its brain was and how smart it might have been.

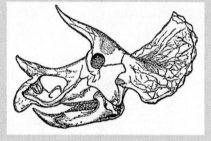

- Fossil footprints showed that duck-billed dinosaurs traveled in large herds.
- Fossils of dinosaur nests and eggs show how they cared for their young.

1. Which information do fossils *not* tell us about an animal?
    a. size
    b. shape
    c. color

2. Fossils can show _____

_____.

3. How can the layer of rock a fossil is found in tell us about when an animal lived?

_____

_____

_____

_____

_____

Name: _____

Paleontologists

Paleontologists are scientists who study the history of life on Earth. Some study fossil plants. Others study fossil animals such as dinosaurs.

Paleontologists work in the field to find fossils. Fossil rock is different from the rock around it. It takes time and skill to remove the rock around a fossil. Paleontologists use tools such as rock hammers, chisels, and brushes to uncover fossils. They record where the fossile was found. They don't want to damage the fossil. They handle them with care:

→ They carefully take them out of the ground.

→ They measure the parts of the fossil.

→ They take pictures with a camera and draw the fossils in a notebook.

→ They clean and study the fossils in labs. They must take care of the fossils.

→ Then, they write about the fossils.

→ They share what they have found with others.

1. What do *paleontologists* study?

    a. how and what animals eat

    b. how old rocks on Earth are

    c. the history of life on Earth

2. What are three things a *paleontologist* does with the fossils he or she finds?

_____

_____

_____

3. If you were a *paleontologist*, what kind of fossils would you like to study? Circle one.

          Plant Fossils   **Animal Fossils**

Explain your choice. _____

_____

Name: _____

The Fossil Record

The **fossil record** is important. It includes all the fossils found in the world. Many animals never became fossils, so the fossil record does not include them.

Fossils tell how living things have changed over millions of years. Did you know that ocean fossils have been found on a mountain? This is **evidence**. It shows that the rocks on the mountain used to be at the bottom of an ocean.

Problems with the Fossil Record

Fossils

➡ **Not very many living things became fossils.**
Fossils only form when things are just right. Animals that lived in water or mud were more likely to become fossils. Big, heavy bones were more likely to become fossils than smaller bones.

➡ **Paleontologists find very few fossils.**
Many fossils came to the surface long ago. They were destroyed by wind and rain. Many more fossils are still deep under the ground. We may never find them. We only find fossils that are near the surface now.

➡ **Paleontologists sometimes make mistakes.**
For a long time, they thought dinosaurs were cold-blooded animals. Now there is more evidence that dinosaurs might have been more like warm-blooded animals.

As scientists discover new evidence, they change how they think about the world.

1. What does the *fossil record* tell us?

   _____

   _____

2. Name two problems with the *fossil record*.

   _____

   _____

   _____

3. What happens when scientists find out that they made a mistake?

   _____

   _____

   _____

Name: _____

What Is Weather?

Every place on Earth has **weather** all the time. Weather is what is happening in the **atmosphere**. The atmosphere is the air around and above us. Air movement, temperature, and water determine the weather.

Air Movement

Air is all around us. Wind is moving air. You can feel and hear the wind and see its effects. It moves things around, such as trees, kites, and your clothes and hair. Wind can make you feel cold, and it can move clouds across the sky.

Temperature

How hot or cold the weather feels is called **temperature**. The weather can feel hot if the Sun is shining and the air is warm and still. When the weather is cold, rain might turn into snow.

Water

A lot of the weather has to do with water in the air. You probably know about the water cycle. Water evaporates, collects in clouds, and falls to Earth. Water that falls from clouds is called **precipitation**. It can be rain, snow, sleet, or hail.

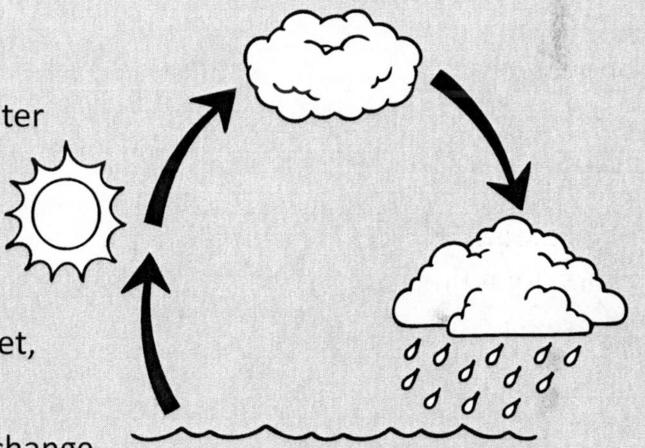

Weather affects the way we live. We change the kinds of clothes we wear depending on the weather. We choose different activities, too. If the weather is cold and snowy, we don't wear a bathing suit and go for a swim! Weather can make us feel good, but it can also be dangerous.

1. What is *weather?*
   a. the water cycle
   b. what happens in the air around us
   c. when the Sun is shining

2. Water that falls from clouds is called _____.

3. How do you know when the wind is blowing?

   _____

   _____

   _____

Name: _____

Weather Can Change

The weather is not the same everywhere at the same time. It is different all over the world. One place can be very hot and windy, while another is very cold and snowy.

Weather in one place can change over time, too. Your day might start out warm and sunny in the morning but change in the afternoon. Dark clouds can roll in, and it will get rainy and windy. The movement of the air and the clouds can change the weather.

Another reason the weather changes is because of the **seasons**. Earth tilts slightly toward the Sun part of the time and slightly away from the Sun the rest of the time. This causes the days to be shorter or longer and brings different kinds of weather.

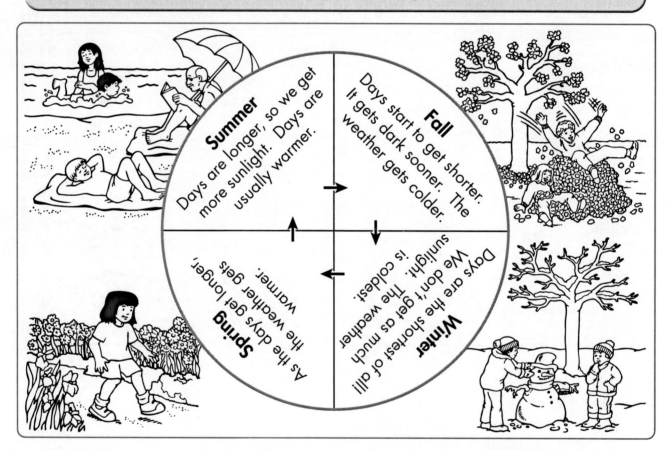

1. The weather   **is**   **is not**   the same everywhere at the same time.

2. Why does Earth have *seasons*?

_____

_____

3. What is your favorite *season*?   **fall**   **winter**   **spring**   **summer**

Why? _____

Name: _____

Types of Weather

There are many different types of weather. Fill in the circle for each type of weather you get where you live.

○ **Sunny:** When there are no clouds in the sky, we say the weather is **clear** and **sunny**. In the spring and summer, a clear day may be warm or hot. In winter, even when the Sun is shining, the temperature can be cold.

○ **Windy:** Wind is formed when warm air and cold air bump into one another. When there is a little bit of wind, we say it is **breezy**. When the air moves quickly, that is **windy** weather. Wind moves clouds from one place to another across the sky.

○ **Cloudy:** Clouds are formed when water droplets gather together in the atmosphere. Clouds can be small and wispy, or big and puffy. When there are just a few clouds, the weather is **partly cloudy**. Lots of clouds can block out the Sun and make the air feel colder. When clouds form low to the ground, it is called fog. If you have been in **foggy** weather, you have been inside a cloud!

○ **Rainy and Snowy:** When water falls from clouds to the ground, we call that **precipitation**. If the weather isn't too cold, water falls as **rain**. When it gets cold enough, rain can turn to **snow**. There are two kinds of frozen raindrops:

   ➡ **Sleet** is frozen rain that falls in the winter.

   ➡ **Hail** is large ice balls that come mostly from thunderstorms.

○ **Stormy:** When you see big, dark clouds and feel strong winds, you can expect **stormy** weather.

○ **Thunderstorms** happen in the summertime. There may be rain or hail and even thunder and lightning.

○ **Winter storms** are very cold and can bring lots of blowing sleet or snow. Be careful in stormy weather!

1. How are *clouds* formed?
   a. Water droplets gather together.
   b. Water freezes.
   c. Water falls to the ground.

2. What causes *wind*? _____

_____

3. What is your favorite kind of weather? _____

   Why? _____

_____

Name: _____

Dangerous Weather

Sometimes, weather can be dangerous. Wind and water sometimes cause damage. Fill in the circle for each type of weather you get where you live.

○ **Lightning:** Lightning is a bolt of electricity formed in a cloud. It can travel inside a cloud, between clouds, and from clouds to the ground. When lightning strikes Earth, it can cause damage and set things on fire.

When you see lightning, you will often hear **thunder**. Thunder does not cause any damage.

○ **Flood:** Usually when it rains, the water flows across the land and into streams and rivers. Then, it travels to a lake or an ocean. When there is too much rain in a short time, it can cause a flood. If too much snow melts very quickly, it can also cause a flood. Water builds up and gets deeper and deeper. The water can get into buildings. It can carry away cars, buildings, and people.

○ **Hurricane:** A hurricane is a huge storm. The wind blows hard enough to flip over cars and tear buildings apart. There is so much rain that it causes flooding. Wind pushes waves of ocean water onto the shore. This enormous storm moves slowly across the land. It can cause damage in a place for a few hours or a few days.

○ **Tornado:** Sometimes, a strong thunderstorm can cause a tornado. Wind swirls around in a circle at speeds of up to 200 miles an hour. A funnel of wind stretches to the ground. Tornadoes can cause a lot of damage. They can tear apart buildings and throw trees in the air.

○ **Blizzard:** A blizzard is a very cold storm. It brings strong winds and snow. The blowing snow makes it hard to see. Blizzards last three hours or more.

1. *Lightning* is _____.
   a. sound in the sky
   b. fire in the atmosphere
   c. electricity formed in a cloud

2. Name two things that can cause damage when the weather is dangerous.

   _____   _____

3. *Lightning* can cause fires. What can a *hurricane* do?

   _____

   _____

Name: _____

Weather Activity

Directions: Name each type of weather and describe it. Explain what you would wear in that type of weather and what you might do.

Word Bank	cloudy	snowy	rainy	stormy

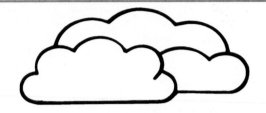

Weather: _____

Description: _____

_____

Clothes: _____

_____

Activities: _____

_____

Weather: _____

Description: _____

_____

Clothes: _____

_____

Activities: _____

_____

Weather: _____

Description: _____

_____

Clothes: _____

_____

Activities: _____

_____

Weather: _____

Description: _____

_____

Clothes: _____

_____

Activities: _____

_____

Name: _____

Weather Forecasting

A **weather forecast** tells what the weather will be like. You can see the weather forecast on TV or hear it on the radio. You can read it online.

Weather scientists study the **atmosphere**. The atmosphere is the air all around Earth. They **forecast**, or make a good guess, about what the weather is going to be.

Scientists need to look at the weather in a large area. They watch storms as they move. They predict where storms will be tomorrow and the next day.

Weather forecasts can help us every day. The forecast can tell us what to wear. If the forecast says it will rain, we know to take an umbrella. If the forecast says it will be hot, we might wear shorts.

Sometimes the weather changes quickly. Weather forecasts can help people get ready for dangerous weather. They can warn people to leave an area before a hurricane or a flood.

TODAY
62 37
morning fog,
partly cloudy

TOMORROW
58 41
rain showers,
cloudy

Weather forecasts are not always right. The weather is always changing. The more scientists learn about the weather, the better their forecasts can be.

1. What is a *weather forecast*?
    a. a warning to leave an area
    b. a good guess about what the weather will be
    c. a program on TV about rain and snow

2. What is the *atmosphere*?
    a. weather
    b. a good guess
    c. the air all around Earth

3. How can a *weather forecast* help you?

    _____

    _____

    _____

Meteorologists

A **meteorologist** is a scientist who studies the weather and the atmosphere. The atmosphere is the air around us. These scientists must learn a lot about science and math. Meteorologists can do different jobs.

Some meteorologists predict what the weather will be. Some go on TV or the radio to explain the weather to people.

Meteorologists look for patterns in the weather. A pattern is something that happens over and over again. When they understand weather patterns, they can predict what the weather will do next.

Some meteorologists do research to learn more about the weather. They might measure how much rain falls or how strong the winds are. They record what they find. They look for patterns.

Some weather study can be dangerous! A few meteorologists study **tornadoes**. They have to get close to the tornadoes to study them. They use special tools and armored cars. They have to be careful!

1. What does a *meteorologist* study?
   a. the atmosphere
   b. patterns in the weather
   c. both **a** and **b**

2. What do *meteorologists* look for to help them predict what the weather will do next?

   _____

   _____

   _____

3. Would you like to be a *meteorologist*?   **Yes**   **No**

   Why or why not? _____

   _____

   _____

Name: _____

Weather Tools

Meteorologists use many different tools to study and predict the weather. Some tools are used on the ground. They send other tools up in airplanes or big balloons. They put some on ships in the oceans. These tools measure what the air, wind, and water are doing in the atmosphere.

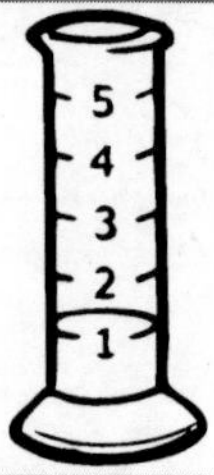	A **rain gauge** measures the amount of rain that falls.	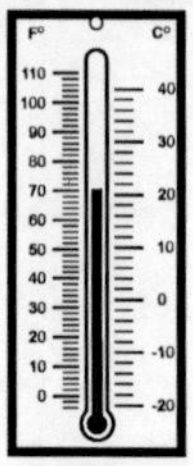	A **thermometer** measures the temperature of the air.
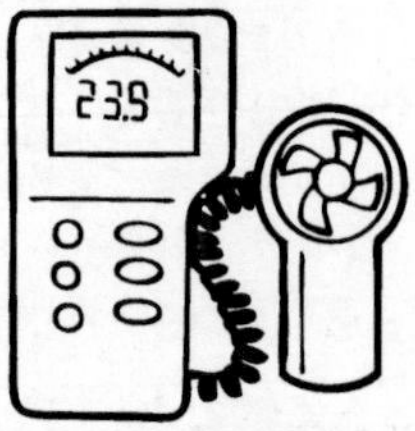	An **anemometer** measures the speed of the wind.		A **weather vane** shows the direction the wind is blowing.

Meteorologists record the **data** that their tools collect. They can use **computers** to study the data on wind speed, temperature, and other things. The computers help them find patterns in the weather.

Weather radar is a tool that can tell where storms are. It gives a picture of how much rain, snow, and wind are in an area. Radar can also tell which direction storms are moving and how fast.

Up in space, **satellites** go around Earth. They take pictures and videos of storms. Meteorologists can use the data to predict where storms will go and how strong they will be.

1. What is another word for *data*?
   a. date
   b. information
   c. tools

2. Which tool measures the speed of the wind?
   a. anemometer
   b. thermometer
   c. wind vane

3. What kind of *data* do meteorologists collect with their tools?

   _____

4. What can *radar* tell meteorologists?

   _____

   _____

Name: _____

Fun with Forecasting

Today, scientists use computers and other tools to predict the weather. How did people know about the weather in the past? Here are some fun ways to check the weather.

- **Check the pinecones.** Pine seeds travel in the wind. On days when it is foggy or rainy, pinecones close up tight. If you see tightly closed pinecones, expect wet weather. When the air is dry, pinecones open up so their seeds can come out. This means the weather will be nicer.

- **Look at the flowers.** At night, dandelion flowers close their petals. They usually open up in the morning, but if it is going to rain, they stay closed. This keeps the pollen inside the flower from washing away. If you see closed dandelion flowers, you should probably grab an umbrella.

- **Listen to the crickets.** Have you heard crickets chirp? Try counting the chirps! Count the number of chirps from one cricket in 15 seconds. Then, add 37. The number you get will be the temperature!

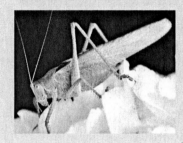

1. If you see closed dandelion flowers in the morning, what could that mean?
   - **a.** rainy weather
   - **b.** sunny weather
   - **c.** dry weather

2. How can you use pinecones to see what the weather will be like?

   _____

   _____

3 | If you listened to a cricket and counted 43 chirps in 15 seconds, what would the temperature be? Do the math here.

Name: _____

Read the Weather Forecast

Monday	Tuesday	Wednesday	Thursday	Friday	Saturday	Sunday
75°	76°	68°	62°	56°	52°	64°
Sunny	Sunny	Partly Cloudy	Cloudy	Cloudy and Windy	Rainy	Partly Cloudy

Directions: Use the weather forecast to answer the questions.

1. What will the temperature be on Thursday? _____

2. Which day will be the warmest? _____

3. Which would be the best day to fly a kite? _____

   Why? _____

   _____

4. On what day will the storm come? _____

5. Will the weather get warmer or cooler during the week? _____

   How can you tell? _____

   _____

6. You have a soccer game outdoors on Saturday. Do you think you will play?   **Yes**   **No**

   Why? _____

   _____

7. What would you wear to school on Friday?

   _____

   _____

Name: _____

What Is Hazardous Weather?

Sometimes, the weather is nice. We can go outside to play. We can take a walk in the rain with an umbrella. We can build a snowman.

But sometimes, the weather is bad. We have to stay inside. It is too hot or too cold to play outside. There could be too much rain or too much snow.

Sometimes, the weather is dangerous. A **weather hazard** is dangerous weather that can hurt people. It can damage property. Weather hazards can be big storms with a lot of rain or snow. Very high or very low temperatures can also be hazards.

You may hear a **weather alert** where you live.

- A **weather watch** means a weather hazard might be coming. You should get ready.

- A **weather advisory** means the weather is bad. You should be careful.

- A **weather warning** tells you that the weather is dangerous. You should take shelter.

---

1. What does *weather hazard* mean?
   a. a big storm
   b. dangerous weather
   c. very high temperatures

2. What kind of *weather alert* is the most serious?
   a. watch
   b. advisory
   c. warning

3. Have you ever had a *weather hazard* where you live? _____

   What was it like? _____

   _____

   _____

Name: _____

Severe Thunderstorms

Storms can happen when a lot of warm air runs into a lot of cold air. Some storms can be dangerous. A **severe thunderstorm** is a dangerous storm. It can bring heavy rain, hail, strong winds, and lightning. These kinds of storms usually happen in the spring and summer.

Thunderstorms can cause other weather hazards, too.

A **flash flood** happens when a lot of rain falls all at once. The water moves very fast. It can carry away people, cars, and even buildings. Pay attention to warnings, and stay away from flash-flood areas.

Hail can be very large in a big storm. Hailstones the size of golf balls or even baseballs can cause a lot of damage. They can damage cars, buildings, and crops on farms. Stay indoors during a hailstorm.

Severe thunderstorms cause a lot of wind. Sometimes, the wind blows in a straight line. But sometimes, the wind swirls around and forms a **tornado**. Very strong and fast winds blow around in a circle. They create a funnel that reaches from a storm cloud to the ground.

Tornados are very dangerous. They can destroy buildings and throw large objects up into the air. Always take shelter during a tornado warning.

1. What is a *flash flood*?
    a. fast-moving water   **b.** water in your house   **c.** a lot of hail all at once

2. What should you do if there is a hailstorm warning?

_____

_____

_____

3. Why are tornadoes dangerous?

_____

_____

_____

Name: _____

Winter Storms

Storms that happen in the winter can be very cold. They often bring snow. Some winter storms can be dangerous.

A **blizzard** is a very large, dangerous snowstorm with strong winds. The wind blows the snow up into the air. It is very hard to see. The snow blows into big **snowdrifts**, or piles. Blizzards last more than three hours, and they sometimes last for days. Stay indoors during a blizzard.

In an **ice storm**, freezing rain falls. When it hits the ground or objects, it freezes into ice. Everything becomes covered in ice. It is not safe to drive because the roads are icy and slippery. Trees can break and fall because the ice on them gets so heavy. The weight of ice can also break power lines. The power often goes out during an ice storm. During an ice storm, stay indoors and try to keep warm.

1. When does an *ice storm* occur?
   a. An ice storm occurs when lots of snow blows in the air.
   b. An ice storm occurs when there is lightning and thunder.
   c. An ice storm occurs when rain freezes on everything.

2. What should you do if there is a dangerous winter storm?

   _____

   _____

   _____

3. What are some ways you can keep warm during a cold storm?

   _____

   _____

   _____

Name: _____

Heat Waves and Drought

Storms usually bring **precipitation** (rain or snow). But what happens when there is not enough rain?

A **drought** occurs when a place does not get enough rain. Plants die. Animals can die, too. Droughts are bad for living things. If you live where there is a drought, try to use less water. Turn off the tap when you are brushing your teeth. Take short showers. Don't waste water!

A **heat wave** happens when the temperature in a place is higher than usual for two or more days. This is also very bad for living things. In a heat wave, you should try to stay cool. Wear light clothing. Don't play or run outside. Drink a lot of water.

Drought

1. Which of these is the word that means *not enough rain*?
   a. drought
   b. heat wave
   c. storm

2. What should you do if there is a *heat wave*?

   _____

   _____

   _____

3. What are some ways you can save water and not waste it?

   _____

   _____

   _____

Name: _____

Preparing for Weather Hazards

We know that weather hazards happen. We need to **prepare**, or get ready, for them.

Flooding happens when water goes in places where it is usually dry. People get prepared in these places. They build **dams** and **channels** to keep water out of cities and neighborhoods. In some places, buildings are lifted up off the ground. They are put on stilts!

Building on stilts

If a flood is coming soon, people can put sandbags in front of houses and other buildings. The sandbags make a wall to keep some water out.

Lightning can be dangerous. Tall buildings often have **lightning rods** on top. The lightning hits the lightning rod. It goes down a wire outside the building and into the ground. The people inside the building are safe.

In places where there can be **droughts**, people save water. They build ponds or lakes called **reservoirs** to collect and save water. People build big pipes and concrete rivers to bring water from where it falls to where it is needed. They drill deep holes called **wells** to get water from under the ground.

Indian stepwell

1. What is a *reservoir*?
   a. a pond or a lake to collect and save water
   b. a house lifted up off the ground on stilts
   c. a deep hole to get water from under the ground

2. What are two ways people *prepare* for floods?

   _____   _____

3. What weather hazards happen where you live?

   _____

   How do people prepare for them? _____

   _____

   _____

Name: _____

Climate vs. Weather

The **atmosphere** is the air all around Earth. Both weather and climate tell you about the atmosphere.

➡ **Weather** tells what is going on with the atmosphere in a place *at one time*. For example, it might be sunny outside where you live. It might be cloudy and windy. It might be raining. The weather can change from day to day.

➡ **Climate** is the pattern of weather in a place over a long time. For example, it might be hot in the summer and cold and snowy in the winter where you live. This happens every year.

Let's say it's a summer day. In the morning, it is hot and sunny. In the afternoon, a big thunderstorm rolls in. There is rain, hail, and lightning. Is this *weather* or *climate*?

It's weather. We are only talking about what is happening in one day.

Now, imagine a place where it is sunny and warm almost all the time. It rains part of the year, and it is dry the other part of the year. Is this *weather* or *climate*?

It's climate. Climate is a **pattern** of weather in a place over a long time.

1. The *atmosphere* is _____.
   a. rain, hail, and lightning
   b. a pattern of weather
   c. the air all around Earth

2. What does *climate* mean? Give an example.

   Climate is _____

   _____

   Example: _____

   _____

3. What is the *atmosphere* like today where you are?

   _____

   _____

Name: _____

Climate or Weather?

Directions: Read each item. Write a **W** on the line in front of the number if it describes *weather*. Write a **C** if it describes *climate*.

_____ 1. I was sad because it rained three days last week and I couldn't play baseball.

_____ 2. Yesterday it was 85° and sunny, so we enjoyed a picnic.

_____ 3. The Sahara desert only gets about 4 inches of rain a year.

_____ 4. The forecast says it will be windy tomorrow.

_____ 5. It is usually cold and snowy here in January.

_____ 6. California gets most of its rain in the winter months.

_____ 7. Josie's town got an inch of rain yesterday.

_____ 8. It is usually cold enough in February that we need gloves and hats.

_____ 9. The wind is blowing from the west at 20 miles per hour.

_____ 10. Today, the temperature in London will be higher than the temperature in Paris.

Name: ____________________________________

Temperature and Precipitation

Scientists study climates. They measure things in the atmosphere. The two most important things are *temperature* and *precipitation*.

Temperature tells how hot or cold the air feels. Scientists study the temperatures in an area.

They look for patterns over a long time:

In warm climates, the air feels warm or hot most of the time.

In other climates, it is hot in the summer and cold in the winter.

In the coldest climates, the air feels cold most of the time.

Precipitation is rain, snow, sleet, or hail that falls from clouds. Scientists measure how much precipitation falls in different places.

They look for patterns over time:

In some climates, very little rain falls at all.

In other climates, there is a lot of rain at one time of the year.

In some climates, a lot of snow falls in the winter, and in others, there is no snow at all.

Patterns in temperature and precipitation help decide the climate of a place.

Rain gauge

1. What is *precipitation*?
   - **a.** climate
   - **b.** rain, snow, sleet, or hail that falls from clouds
   - **c.** how hot or cold the air feels

2. What is *temperature*?

____

____

3. What helps define the climate of a place?

____

____

Name: _____

Climate Zones

On Earth, there are three main climate **zones**, or areas.

Polar: The polar zones are at the top and bottom of Earth. The way Earth is tilted means the Sun doesn't warm these areas as much. Most of the time, they are covered in snow or ice.

➡ The pattern in polar areas is that they are freezing cold most of the time.

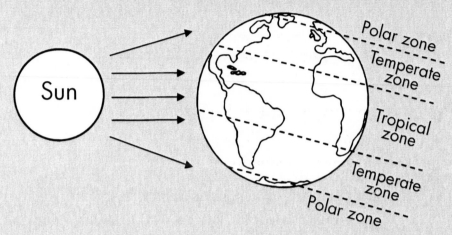

Tropical: The tropical zones are around the equator. In these zones, the Sun shines a long time each day, all year long. It is very warm.

➡ The pattern in tropical zones is hot and rainy almost every day.

Temperate: The temperate zones are in between the polar and tropical zones. The Sun warms these areas in the summers. It is not as warm in the winters.

➡ The pattern in these areas is warmer in the spring and summer. It is cooler in the fall and winter.

1. Where are the polar zones?
   a. the top and bottom of Earth
   b. the middle of Earth
   c. between the polar and tropical zones

2. Why are the tropical zones so warm?

   _____

   _____

3. Look at the diagram of climate zones. Which climate zone do you live in?

   _____

Name: _____

Climate Data

Earth has three types of **climate zones**:

➡ The **polar** climate zones are cold all the time.

➡ The **temperate** climate zones have warm or hot summers and cold winters.

➡ The **tropical** climate zones are warm all the time.

Temperature °F	
January	23
February	26
March	37
April	51
May	62
June	73
July	78
August	77
September	66
October	55
November	39
December	28

Directions: Use the **Temperature Data Table** and the **Monthly Temperatures Line Graph** to answer the questions.

1. Use the data table to fill in the line graph. **January through March** has been done for you.

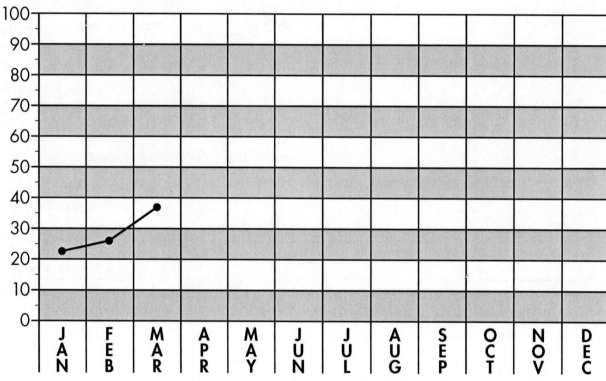

2. What is the difference between the highest and lowest temperatures? _____

3. Look at the temperature graph. Which climate zone do you think this place is in? Circle your choice.

Polar Zone	**Temperate Zone**	**Tropical Zone**

Why? _____

_____

Name: _____

States of Matter

Everything around you is made of **matter**. Kittens, rocks, rain, and air are made of matter. Your body is made of matter. Matter is anything that takes up space. The amount of matter in an object is its **mass**. The way that matter takes up space is called its **state**.

There are three states of matter: **solid**, **liquid**, and **gas**.

All matter is made of tiny bits or **particles**. When scientists want to find out about the state of matter, they look at what the particles in it are doing.

Solid	Liquid	Gas

In a **solid**, the particles stay very close together. They don't move around much at all. These things are solids:

In a **liquid**, the particles stay close together, but they can move around. These things have liquids in them:

In a **gas**, the particles can spread apart. They move around a lot in all directions. These things have gases inside them:

1. How do the *particles* in a *solid* behave?

_____

_____

2. How do the particles in a *liquid* behave differently from the particles in a *solid*?

_____

_____

3. How do the particles in a *gas* behave differently from the particles in a *liquid*?

_____

_____

Name: _____

Solids

Solids can be any shape or size. Trees, toenails, turtles, televisions, and toys are all solids. Solids can be hard, like diamonds or soft, like cloths. They can be small, like grains of sand, or huge like mountains.

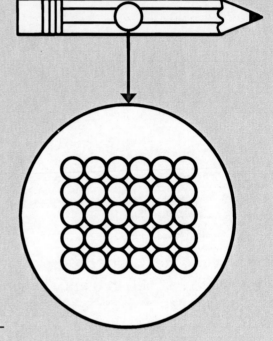

In a solid, the particles are close together and don't move very much. The particles are arranged in a **structure** or a pattern. They have a very strong **attraction** to one another. Have you ever built something with toy bricks that snap together? That's a lot like the particles in a solid.

If you set a solid down, it will keep its shape. When you put your pencil on your desk, does it change shape? No. It is a solid. So is this paper. Their particles stay together in the same structure.

You can change the shape of a solid—you can cut or crumple up paper or sharpen a pencil—but a solid won't change shape on its own.

1. How do you know if something is a *solid*?
    a. You can cut it.
    b. It keeps its shape.
    c. You can snap it together.

2. *Solids* cannot change _____ on their own.

3. Name three *solids* you can see right now. Draw them.

Name: _____

Liquids

Liquids can *pour*, *flow*, *drip*, and *splash*. Water, milk, juice, syrup, glue, and paint are all liquids.

In a liquid, the particles are close together, but they can move around and slide past one another. Their attraction to one another is not as strong as in a solid. This is why liquids **flow**.

Liquids do not keep their shape. The particles stay close to one another, but they can move around. Have you ever spilled a liquid? What happens? It spreads out as flat as it can get. Some liquids flow very easily, such as water. Others flow slowly, such as ketchup.

Because liquids flow, you can pour them. They always flow down since they are pulled by gravity. They take the shape of whatever container they are in. This is why the same amount of water can fill up a tall glass or a wide bowl, or it can spread out on your floor if you spill it.

Liquids cannot be **compressed**, or squeezed. Imagine that you fill up a glass with water. Once it is full, you cannot squeeze the water to make it smaller and add more. If you add more, it will just spill over the top of the glass.

1. Which of these can you not do to a *liquid*?
   a. pour it
   b. splash it
   c. cut it

2. Give three examples of *liquids*.

   _____

   _____

   _____

3. Explain why *liquids* do not keep their shape.

   _____

   _____

   _____

Name: _____

Gases

Gases are hard to describe because you can't usually see them. Sometimes, you can feel them, though. Have you ever felt air blowing? Air is a mixture of gases that is all around us. Air is all around Earth.

There are many different types of gases in air, such as oxygen, carbon dioxide, and water vapor. There is air in the tires of a car and air in a basketball.

The tiny particles in gases are far apart. They bounce around very quickly. They aren't connected to one another.

Gases, such as liquids, do not have their own shape. A gas will always take the shape of its container. The gas does not sit in the bottom of the container like a liquid. It spreads out evenly all around the container.

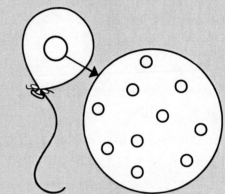

To keep a gas in a container, you need to close the container. If you leave it open, the gas will spread out. Think of the air in a balloon. If you don't tie off the balloon, the air gets out.

Gas particles are not like liquid particles. Liquid particles go down. Gas can go up. It can move sideways. The particles spread out to take up all the space they can.

Gas can be squeezed into a smaller space. Imagine you are pumping up a basketball. You fill it with air. Then, you can pump even more air into it. The gas particles get closer together to make more room.

1. The particles in a *gas* are _____.
   a. spread apart from one another
   b. close together
   c. strongly attached to one another

2. Air is a _____ of gases.

3. What will happen if you open a container full of a gas?

   _____

   _____

   _____

Name: _____

Phase Changes

Matter can change **states**. Think about water. It can be a liquid, a solid, or a gas.

When water is cold enough, it **freezes**. It becomes a **solid**. We call it **ice**. When it is not too cold and not too hot, water is **liquid**. If it gets hot enough, water changes into a gas called **water vapor**. Water can change back and forth between different states as it gets hotter or colder.

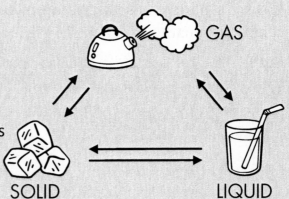

Have you learned about the water cycle? On Earth, water changes states as it moves around. Liquid water in oceans, lakes, and rivers **evaporates**. This water changes to water vapor—a gas. Water vapor collects in clouds and turns to liquid. The liquid can fall as rain. If it is cold enough, the liquid becomes solid ice and falls as snow or hail.

Other types of matter can change, too. But we don't usually see all three states like we do with water.

1. For each item, write the state of matter: *solid*, *liquid*, or *gas*.

   cookie _____   **rain** _____

   a sponge _____   **oxygen** _____

   water vapor _____   **shampoo** _____

2. Fill in the blanks to explain how water changes from one state to another.

   When water changes from a solid to a liquid, it _____.

   When water changes from a liquid to a gas, it _____.

   When water changes from a liquid to a solid, it _____.

3. Describe the different states of matter in a glass of soda with ice cubes in it.

   Soda is a _____.

   Bubbles in soda are _____.

   Ice cubes in soda are _____.

Name: _____

What Is Force?

What is a **force**? A force is a push or a pull that changes an object's **shape** or **position**.

We see and feel forces around us all the time. You use force when you brush your teeth, walk to class, or write with a pencil. Forces make cars go, make rain fall, and make the Moon move around Earth.

A **push** is a force that moves something away.

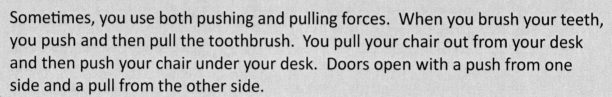

    You can push a button, a stroller or a swing.

    You can push a toy car with your hand.

    You can push a skateboard with your foot.

    When you kick or throw a ball, you are using a pushing force.

A **pull** is a force that moves something closer.

    You can pull a book from the shelf or pull up a zipper.

    You pull on socks and mittens.

    When you pick up a book from your desk or brush your hair, you are using a pulling force.

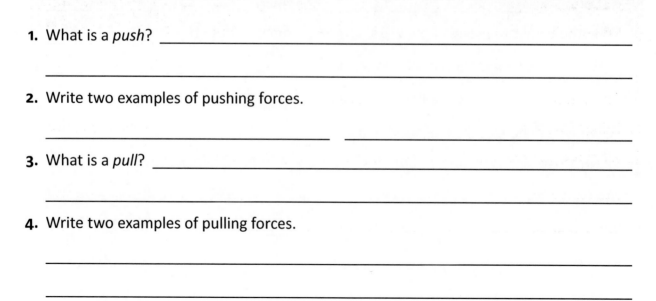

Sometimes, you use both pushing and pulling forces. When you brush your teeth, you push and then pull the toothbrush. You pull your chair out from your desk and then push your chair under your desk. Doors open with a push from one side and a pull from the other side.

---

1. What is a *push*? _____

_____

2. Write two examples of pushing forces.

_____ _____

3. What is a *pull*? _____

_____

4. Write two examples of pulling forces.

_____

_____

Name: _____

Force and Motion

You can make things move. A ball moves when you kick it. The pages of a book move when you turn them, and you move your pencil when you are writing.

Things do not move by themselves. When something is not moving, we say it is **at rest**. Things stay at rest unless a **force** (a push or a pull) makes them move.

Try This: Set your pencil on your desk, and do not touch it. Does it move?

No. It cannot move by itself. Your pencil is at rest.

Now, push your pencil gently with your finger. Did it move?

Yes. You applied force (a push) to the pencil with your finger, and it moved.

What can happen when a force makes something move? Here are some ways that force can affect motion.

Force can make something **start moving** or **stop moving**.

Example: You can start a toy moving by throwing it to your dog. When your dog catches the toy, it stops moving.

Force can make something **speed up** or **slow down**.

Example: A driver pushes the gas pedal on a car to make it speed up. They push the brakes to make it slow down.

Force can make something **change direction**.

Example: When a baseball player hits a moving ball with a bat, it makes the ball change direction.

1. Which of these means that something is not moving?
   a. in force   **b.** at rest   **c.** in motion

2. Things stay at rest unless a _____ makes them move.

3. What are two ways that *force* can make something move?

   _____

   _____

   _____

Name: _____

What Is Motion?

Motion is a change in place or position. When something moves, we say that it is "in motion." Place your pencil on your desk. Now, push it a little with your finger. It changes its **position** on the desk. The pencil is in a different place, but the desk didn't move. That's how you know that the pencil moved.

Motion has both speed and direction.

- **Speed** is how fast something moves. A snail moves slowly. A race car moves quickly.

- **Direction** is where something goes when it moves. You can run in a straight line or a zigzag. You can turn in a circle. You can walk up or down stairs.

When you see a car driving down the road, it is easy to see it moving because it moves quickly. You can see that it does not stay in the same position. Sometimes things move slowly, so it is harder to tell if they are moving.

How do you know that the hands on a clock are moving? If you watch a clock, you might not see them move because they are moving so slowly. So, you look at the clock and remember where the hands are. Some time later, you look again, and the hands are pointing to different numbers. That is how you know they moved.

1. What is *motion*?

   a. a measure of speed   **b.** a sense of direction   **c.** a change in position

2. How can you tell if something is moving?

   _____

   _____

3. Name two things that should move slowly.

   _____   _____

4. What is something you like to do quickly? _____

   Why? _____

   _____

Name: _____

Force and Shape

Force can make things change **shape**.

Try This: Put one hand face up on your desk. Use one finger from your other hand to gently poke your palm. You are applying **force** to your palm. What happens? Your hand doesn't change position, but it does change shape just a little bit. It gets a dent where you pushed on it, but the dent doesn't stay.

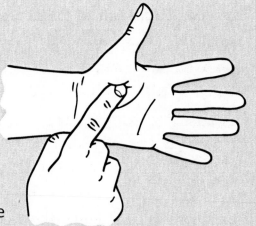

Have you ever played with clay? You apply force by pushing and pulling it. It changes shape.

Here are some more examples of how you can use force to change an object's shape:

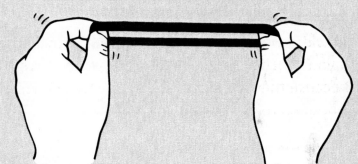

- Squeeze a sponge.
- Stretch a rubber band.
- Fold paper.
- Crush a cracker.
- Blow up a balloon.

1. Force can make things change _____.
   a. position
   b. shape
   c. both **a** and **b**

2. To make something change *shape*, you need to apply _____.

3. Name two ways you can use force to change an object's shape.

_____

_____

_____

_____

Name: _____

Strength of Forces

It takes **energy** to apply a force to something. Depending on how much energy they use, forces can be different strengths.

It takes more energy to push or pull something farther or faster. If you use just a little bit of force to throw a ball, it won't go very far or very fast. If you use a strong force to throw a ball, it goes farther and faster.

Try This: Put your pencil on your desk. Use your finger to push your pencil with a little bit of force. Now, push it with a bit more force. Did you see a difference? When you push with more force, it moves farther and faster.

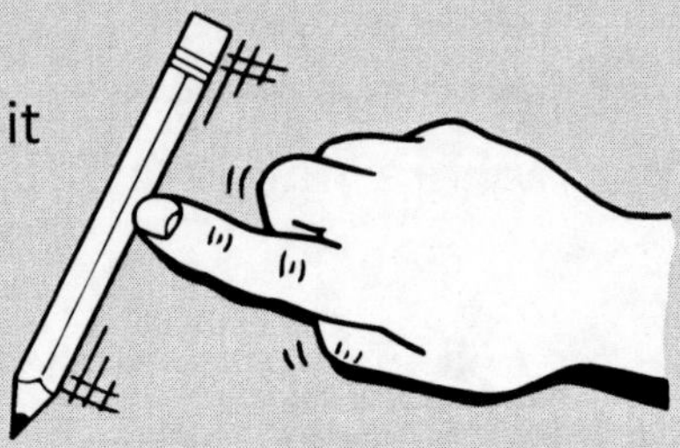

It takes more energy to push or pull something heavy. You need to use a stronger force. Which would you need to use more force to move—an empty chair or a chair with your friend in it? You would need to push harder to move the chair with your friend in it.

Try This: Place your pencil and a large book on your desk. Push each one with your finger to make it move a bit. Which was harder to push? You need to use a stronger force to push the book because it is heavier.

1. If you use a strong force to throw a ball, _____.
    a. it only goes a little way
    b. it goes farther and faster
    c. it won't go very far or very fast

2. It takes a _____ force to move something heavy.
    a. weak
    b. fast
    c. strong

3. Name something it would take only a little bit of force to move.

_____

4. Name something it would take a lot of force to move.

_____

Name: _____

Balanced and Unbalanced Forces

There is almost always more than one force acting on something. If the forces acting on an object are **unbalanced**, or different from one another, the object will move or change shape.

Try This: First, place a book on your desk in front of you. With one hand, push the book a little bit. What happens?

You put force on just one side of the book. The force was unbalanced, so the book moved.

Sometimes, the forces acting on an object are **balanced**. They are the same strength pushing or pulling in opposite directions. Then, the object does not move.

Try This: Put one hand on each side of the book. Push with both hands toward one another. Push the same amount with each hand. What happens?

If you push equally with both hands, the book will not move. The forces are balanced.

Directions: Choose words from the Word Bank to complete the sentences.

Word Bank	balanced	opposite	strength	unbalanced

1. When forces acting on an object are _____,

   the object will not move.

2. When forces acting on an object are _____,

   the object will move.

3. *Balanced* forces are the same _____ pushing or pulling

   in _____ directions.

Name: _____

Unbalanced Forces

When the **forces** on something are **balanced**, the object will not move. If the forces acting on it are **unbalanced**, the object will move.

Look at this picture of two people playing tug-of-war. The forces are balanced. Each person is pulling on the rope with the same force. The rope is not moving.

Look at this picture. One person is pulling harder than the other person. What will happen?

The forces are unbalanced. The rope moves toward the person that is pulling with more force.

Directions: For each picture, write *balanced* if the forces are balanced, or *unbalanced* if the forces are not balanced. Then, write how you know.

1	The forces are _____
	because _____
	_____ .

2	The forces are _____
	because _____
	_____ .

3	The forces are _____
	because _____
	_____ .

4	The forces are _____
	because _____
	_____ .

Name: _____

Gravity

Why do things fall down? Why don't they stay in the same place, floating in the air? Why don't they go up?

Try This: Hold your pencil a few inches above your desk, and let it go. What happens?

Things fall because of a force called **gravity**. Gravity is a pulling force. We can't see gravity, but we can feel it. Gravity on Earth pulls everything toward the center of the planet. It is a force that is always acting on everything around us.

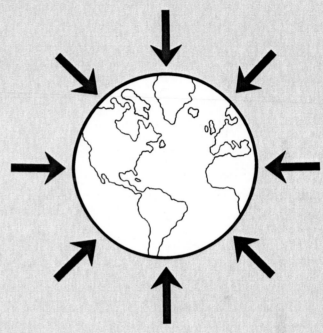

The more mass something has, the more gravity pulls things toward it. Gravity on Earth is strong because Earth is very big. Gravity keeps everything on Earth from floating off into space. People, animals, trees, and mountains stay on Earth. The air stays all around Earth. It does not float away.

Earth's gravity pulls on the Moon and keeps it from leaving its orbit around Earth!

1. Which of these is true?
   a. Gravity is a pushing force.
   b. Gravity is a pulling force.
   c. Gravity is a visible force.

2. *Gravity* on Earth is strong because _____

   _____.

3. *Gravity* pulls everything on Earth toward _____

   _____.

Name: _____

Gravity and Weight

Imagine you have a bowling ball and a balloon that are the same size. Which is heavier?

The bowling ball is heavier. It has more **weight**. But what is weight?

An object's weight is a measure of the **force of gravity** pulling on that object. The force of gravity pulls harder on a bowling ball than a balloon because the bowling ball has more mass.

The more mass an object has, the more gravity it has. The Moon has a lot less mass than Earth. The Moon has gravity, but not as much as Earth.

When astronauts went to the Moon, they could tell that gravity was different. The Moon's gravity did not pull on them as strongly as gravity on Earth pulled them. They did not weigh as much. The astronauts had fun running and bouncing in the Moon's weaker gravity.

1. What is *gravity*?
   a. Gravity is a weight.
   b. Gravity is a force.
   c. Gravity is a planet.

2. The Moon has less mass than Earth, so the Moon has _____ gravity.

3. What is *weight*?

   _____

   _____

4. Astronauts found out that gravity was different on the Moon. How was gravity different?

   _____

   _____

Name: _____

Balancing Gravity

You are probably sitting in a chair. If you stay very still, are there forces acting on you? Yes! Gravity is pulling you down. But you are not moving. Why aren't you falling as gravity pulls you?

Gravity is pulling you down. But the force of the chair is pushing you up with an equal force. You are not moving because the forces are **balanced**.

Look at this paper on your desk. Gravity is pulling on it. Why is it not falling? Because the force of the desk is pushing up. The forces are **balanced**, so the paper doesn't move.

Try This: Put your hand on the desk. Lift your hand up. Put your hand back down. When your hand is on the desk, gravity is pulling your hand down and the desk is pushing your hand up. The forces are **balanced**, so your hand doesn't move.

If gravity is pulling your hand down, how did you lift it up? The force of your muscles overcame the pull of gravity! The force of your muscles and the force of gravity were **unbalanced**, so your hand moved up. When you relaxed your muscles and let your hand drop, the forces became balanced again.

1. When you sit still in a chair, the forces acting on you are _____.
   a. balanced
   b. unbalanced

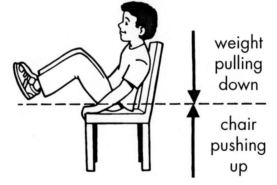

weight
pulling
down

chair
pushing
up

2. If you want to lift your pencil up off your desk, which force needs to be stronger?
   a. gravity
   b. your muscles
   c. the pencil

3. Place a book on your desk. Explain why it stays there and does not move.

   _____

   _____

   _____

Name: _____

Friction

Friction is a force that happens when two things rub against one another.

Try This: Rub your hands together. Rub your hand on your desk. You can feel the friction.

What causes friction? Even though your desk looks smooth, it has very small bumps and cracks on it. Your hand has bumps and cracks, too. When two things rub together, the bumps on each one run into one another. That's what causes friction.

Some surfaces are bumpier than others. When something moves across a smooth surface, there is less friction. The rougher the surface, the higher the friction. Try rubbing your hand on different surfaces such as a book, your clothes, your chair, and the floor. Rub your hands together. Can you feel the difference in the friction on different surfaces?

1. What is *friction*?
   a. a rough surface with bumps and cracks
   b. a force that happens when two things rub together
   c. very small bumps on the surface of an object

2. Which type of surface causes less *friction* when things move across it?
   a. smooth　　　　　　　　b. rough　　　　　　　　c. bumpy

3. Rub your hand on a surface. Name the surface and describe what the *friction* feels like.

   The friction on the _____ surface

   feels like _____.

Name: _____

Friction and Motion

Friction always works in the **opposite** direction of motion. It makes moving things slow down or stop. For instance, when you push a book across your desk, friction works in the opposite direction to keep the book from moving. You have to push with more force than the friction force.

When you are wearing socks, it is easy to slide across a smooth floor. There is very little friction. But if one or both of the surfaces is rough, there is more friction. It is harder to slide in shoes than in socks. And it is harder to slide on a rug than on a smooth floor. The more friction there is, the more force you need to move something.

Rub your hand on your desk. Now, push down harder while rubbing. The friction is stronger. It is harder to move your hand. Friction makes it harder to slide heavier things.

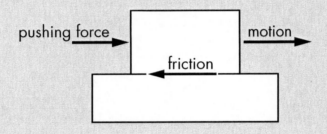

1. Which of these statements is true?

   a. It is easier to slide something on a rough surface than on a smooth surface.

   b. It is easier to slide something lighter than something heavier.

   c. It is easier to slide something if you push down hard on it.

2. Friction works in the _____ direction of motion.

3. Pretend you need to slide a very heavy box from one side of a room to the other. The room has tile on some parts of the floor and carpet on other parts. Which surface would be easier to slide the box on?

   _____

   Why? _____

   _____

Name: _____

Air Resistance

Try This: Hold your pencil out in front of you. Let go! What happened?

Now, hold a sheet of paper out in front of you. Make the flat side face the floor. Let go! What happened? Why did the paper fall slower than the pencil?

What's going on here? It has to do with something that is all around you, but you can't see it. Do you know what it is? It's air!

Air is made of tiny parts called **molecules**. As gravity pulls your paper toward the floor, the surface of the paper bumps against a lot of air molecules on the way down. That is a form of friction called **air resistance**. It is a friction force between an object and the air.

Why did the paper fall more slowly than the pencil? Think about the shape of the pencil and the shape of the paper. The pencil doesn't bump against as many air molecules as the paper does on the way down.

Air resistance is not as strong as gravity. It doesn't usually stop things from falling. But it can slow things down. Parachutes use air resistance to help people fall more slowly and safely than they would on their own.

1. Air is made of _____.

    a. friction

    b. air resistance

    c. molecules

2. Air resistance is a friction force between an

   object and _____.

3. On the picture to the right, draw an arrow showing which way gravity is pulling. Label the arrow "gravity."

4. Draw another arrow showing which way air resistance is pushing the parachute. Label the arrow "air resistance."

Name: _____

Interpreting Data: Friction

Jill and Moses are doing an experiment. They want to find out what kind of surface will help their car go the farthest. They made a ramp. They put different surfaces at the bottom of the ramp. They rolled a toy car down the ramp and recorded how far the car went each time.

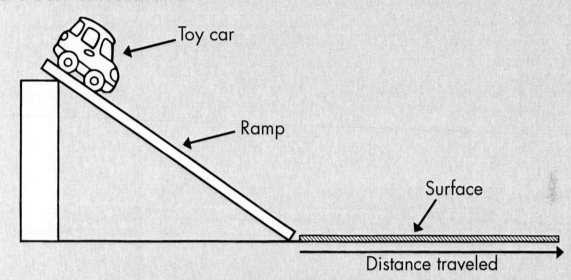

Toy car

Ramp

Surface

Distance traveled

Use the data table below to answer the questions.

Surface	Distance
cardboard	23 inches
carpet	5 inches
sandpaper	7 inches
tile	26 inches

1. On which surface did the car travel farthest? _____

2. On which surface did the car travel the shortest distance? _____

3. How much farther did the car travel on tile than on carpet? _____

4. Which surface do you think had the least friction with the car's wheels?

_____

What is your evidence?

_____

_____

Name: _____

The Feather and the Hammer

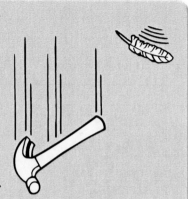

Imagine dropping a feather and a hammer from the same height at the same time. Which would hit the ground first? Use what you know about **air resistance** to make a good guess.

The feather has more air resistance, so the hammer would fall faster and hit the ground first. But why does the feather fall more slowly? The feather falls more slowly because of air resistance. The feather floats down. It is light and flat.

Now, what would happen if there was no air? Remember, gravity pulls on all things equally, no matter what their mass is.

We know what would happen because an astronaut tried this experiment on the Moon! Commander David Scott dropped a feather and a hammer at the same time. Because there is no air on the Moon, there is no air resistance. The feather and the hammer hit the surface of the Moon at the same time. It did not matter that the hammer was heavier!

1. A feather falls slowly on Earth because of _____.
   a. air resistance
   b. gravity
   c. weight

2. Would a parachute help astronauts land safely on the Moon?   **Yes**   **No**

   Why or why not? _____

   _____

3. If you went to the Moon, what two things would you drop to test for *air resistance*?

   _____   _____

   What do you think would happen?

   _____

   _____

Name: _____

Magnets

You can't see gravity, but you know it's there. How do you know? You can feel gravity pulling you.

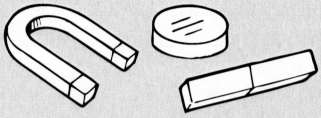

There is another kind of force that you can't see, but you can see it working. It's called **magnetism**. You have probably seen or held a magnet. Magnets are made of metal. They can be any shape or size, but the ones you use in school are usually shaped like a bar or a horseshoe.

The force of magnetism can pull some things toward a magnet. When a magnet pulls, we say it **attracts**.

Magnetic force can also push some things away from a magnet. When a magnet pushes, we say it **repels**.

A magnet does not have to be touching something to attract or repel it. You can hold a metal paper clip near a magnet, and you will feel it being attracted. This might seem like magic, but it is **magnetic force**!

The area around the magnet where it has force is called its **magnetic field**. Magnetic force is all around a magnet, but it is strongest at the ends. The stronger the magnet, the farther away its force can work. Magnetic force can even work through some things, such as wood, glass, or water.

1. *Magnetism* is _____.
      a. a force   **b.** an idea   **c.** a metal

2. When something is pulled toward a magnet, we say it is _____.

3. When something is pushed away from a magnet, we say it is _____.

4. Look at the magnets. Use **repelling** or **attracting** to label each picture.

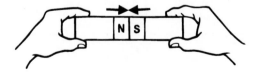 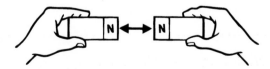

_____   _____

Name: _____

North and South Poles

Every magnet has two **poles**. The magnetic force comes out of the **north pole**. It goes around the magnet and goes in the **south pole**. Magnetism tries to make things line up in a straight line along the poles.

When you put two magnets near one another, their magnetic fields put force on one another.

➡ Two poles that are opposite, a north and a south, will **attract** or pull toward one another.

➡ Two poles that are the same, a north and a north or a south and a south, will **repel** or push away from one another.

Earth is a giant magnet. The North and South Poles of our planet are magnetic poles. But their names are backwards! The place we call the North Pole is actually the south magnetic pole of Earth. This is how a compass works. The needle in a compass is magnetized. It will always point toward the poles. We call the south magnetic pole of Earth the "North Pole" because that is where the north end of a compass needle always points.

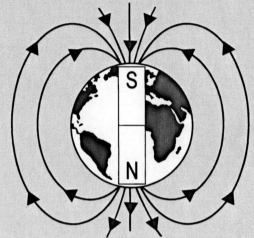

1. Poles that are _____ will *attract* toward one another.
   a. the same
   b. opposite

2. What would happen if you put the north poles of two magnets near one another?

   _____

   _____

3. The north end of a compass needle should be attracted to which pole of Earth?
   a. North
   b. South

4. The south magnetic pole of Earth is called the _____ Pole.

Name: _____

Attract or Repel?

For each picture, write **attract** if the magnets will pull toward one another. Write **repel** if the magnets will push away from one another. Draw arrows to show the movement.

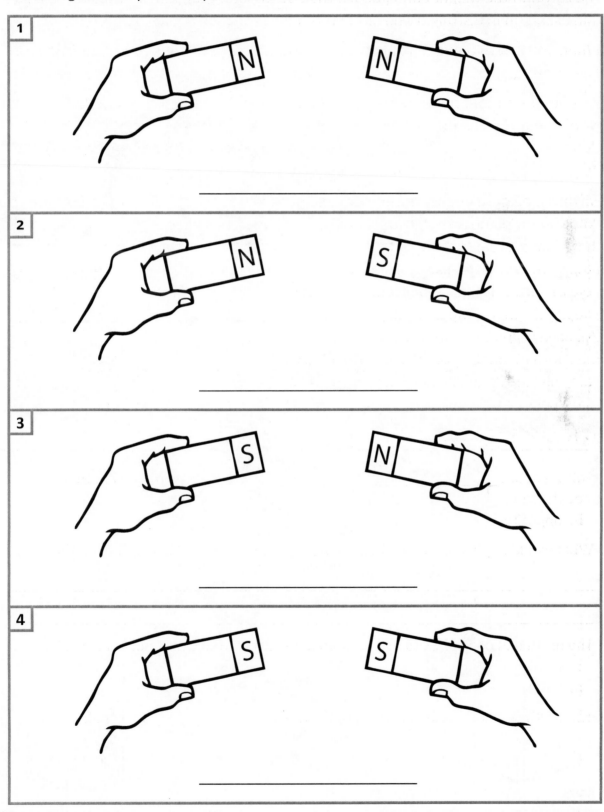

1 | N ... N

_____

2 | N ... S

_____

3 | S ... N

_____

4 | S ... S

_____

Name: _____

What Is Magnetic?

Magnetic force does not work on everything. It does not work on a lot of metals. A magnet won't attract to aluminum soda cans but will attract to tin cans. It won't attract to pots, pans, or coins. A magnet only works on some metals.

Iron is a metal. Magnets work on iron. If something has enough iron in it, it could attract a magnet. Paper clips, scissors, or pins might be attracted to a magnet.

You can stick a magnet to some refrigerator doors but not to others. Dollar bills have iron in the ink printed on them. If a magnet is really strong, it will attract a dollar bill! Some breakfast cereals also have iron in them. Could they be magnetic? They could be magnetic if there is enough iron.

Magnetic force does not work on things that are not metal. Magnets won't attract wood or paper. They will not attract glass, rubber, or plastic.

Directions: Circle the things that *might* be attracted to a magnet. Put an **X** through the things that a magnet would *not* be attracted to.

Name: _____

Magnets Can Do Work

Magnets are used in lots of things you see every day. They can hold a cabinet closed. They can hold a list on the refrigerator. They can be used in things such as computers, telephones, and earphones. A machine called an MRI uses magnets to see inside people. This helps doctors see what is wrong when someone is sick.

Farmers feed magnets to cows. Yes, they really do! The magnets keep the cows healthy. Sometimes, cows eat small bits of metal. These little metal pieces can make them sick. To help, farmers put a small magnet, about the size of your finger, into a young cow's stomach.

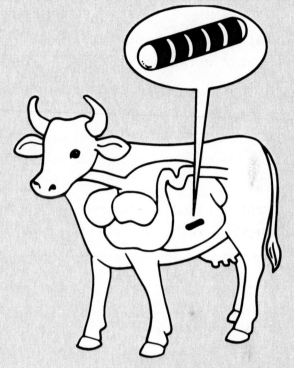

The magnet stays in the cow for the rest of its life. The magnet attracts and holds the small bits of metal the cow eats. This keeps the metal from hurting the cow. If farmers want to check if a cow already has a magnet, they use a compass!

1. What are two ways you use magnets?

_____

_____

2. What do the magnets in an MRI machine help doctors do?

_____

_____

3. Why do farmers put magnets in cows?

_____

_____

_____

Name: _____

Sir Isaac Newton

Sir Isaac Newton was a scientist who lived a long time ago. He studied science and math. Many of his discoveries are still important to scientists today.

Facts About Isaac Newton

- His mother wanted him to be a farmer. He didn't like that idea! He worked as a waiter so he could make money to go to college.

- He studied how things move. He came up with three **laws**, or rules, about motion. These laws still help us today.

- He used math to understand gravity. His math helps explain how the planets in our solar system move around the Sun.

- He also tried many things that did not work out. For example, he tried to turn different metals into gold.

- He was the first scientist to be made a knight by the Queen of England. That is why he is called Sir Isaac Newton.

- Sir Isaac Newton is considered one of the most important scientists who ever lived. Newton's work is so important that the units for measuring force are called **newtons**!

1. What is the main idea of this passage?
    a. Sir Isaac Newton lived a long time ago.
    b. Sir Isaac Newton's work is important.
    c. Sir Isaac Newton tried to turn metals into gold.

2. The units for measuring force are called _____.

3. Sir Isaac Newton did some very important work. But some of the things he did were not successful. Have you ever done an experiment or tried to build something that didn't work the way you wanted? Write about it.

_____

_____

_____

_____

_____

Name: _____

Newton's First Law of Motion

Newton's first law of motion has two parts. The first part says:

An object at rest will stay at rest unless a force acts on it.

We observe this all the time. If you set a rock on the ground in front of you and no one touches it, does it move? No, because there is no unbalanced force to make it move.

The second part is a bit trickier. It says:

An object in motion will keep moving the same way unless a force acts on it.

If you push the rock with your foot it will slide or roll across the ground. But after a bit it stops moving. This is because the forces of **friction** and **gravity** are slowing it down and causing it to stop moving.

Imagine the rock is out in space, away from the gravity of any other object. If the rock was pushed, it would start moving. It would keep moving until a different force acted upon it.

The basic idea of Newton's first law is that an object will keep doing what it is doing unless a force acts on it. If it is sitting still, it will stay still. If it is moving, it will keep moving the same way.

1. Newton's first law says that if an object is not moving it will _____.
   a. stay still unless a force acts on it
   b. move slowly and then stop
   c. roll until gravity and friction stop it

2. If you roll a ball across the classroom, what force or forces will make it stop moving?

   _____

3. Look at the picture and think about Newton's first law of motion. What will happen to the rock rolling down the hill when it hits the boulder? Why?

   _____

   _____

   _____

   _____

Name: _____

Newton's Second Law of Motion

Newton's second law of motion is about *how much force* is needed to move something. The law explains that you need more force to move things with more mass.

Things with more mass are harder to move. Your backpack is harder to lift when it has more books in it.

Think about it: Would it be harder to pull an empty wagon or a wagon with a baby elephant in it?

➡ You would need to use a lot more **force** to move the wagon with the elephant. Why? Because it has more mass.

You also know that the more force you apply to something, the faster it will move. Let's say you gave the baby elephant's wagon a push and it moved slowly. What would happen if five of your friends helped you push?

➡ That would put more force on the wagon, and it would move faster.

1. Which would you need the most force to move?
   a. a frog in a wagon
   b. a dog in a wagon
   c. a hippo in a wagon

2. If you wanted to kick a ball from one end of a field to the other, would you kick it very softly?   **Yes**   **No**

   Why, or why not? _____

   _____

3. If you were to push a soccer ball and a bowling ball with the same amount of force, which would move faster?

   Why? _____

   _____

Name: _____

Newton's Third Law of Motion

Newton's third law of motion is about how two different objects put force on one another. It says:

For every action force, there is an equal and opposite reaction force.

Have you ever blown up a balloon and then let it go? What happens?

First, the air rushes out of the neck of the balloon in one direction. That is an **action** force.

Then, the balloon moves in the other direction. That is the **equal and opposite reaction** force.

Try This: Stand up. Jump into the air. When you jump, your feet push on the ground. The ground pushes back with the same amount of force in the opposite direction. This is why you move up, in the opposite direction of your push.

What happens if you stand on a skateboard and push the ground with your foot? You put force on the ground. The ground puts force on you in the opposite direction. You roll away!

1. Newton's third law says that for every action there is a(n) _____ reaction.
   a. equal and opposite
   b. different and opposite
   c. equal and sideways

2. If you bounce a ball on the ground, the ball pushes on the ground. The ground puts equal and opposite force on the ball. Draw two arrows to show which way the forces push.

3. Explain how Newton's third law works when you push off on a skateboard.

   _____

   _____

   _____

Name: _____

Observe, Measure, and Predict Force

Scientists who study how things move are called **physicists**. Some things they study are as small as atoms. Other things are large, such as planets.

Physicists watch how things move. They look for **patterns** in the way that things happen. A pattern is when something happens over and over again in the same way. When something happens in a pattern, you can **predict** what will happen next.

Directions: Look at the two patterns of motion. *Predict* what will happen next in each case. Circle the arrow showing the direction each object will go next.

1.

2.
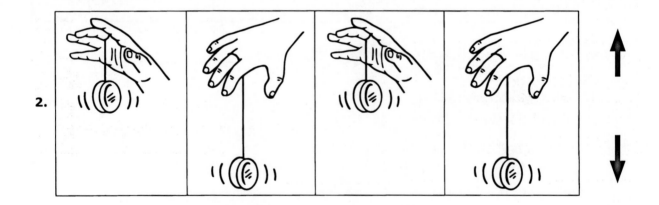

3. Can you think of any other things that move in a *pattern*? Write them here.

_____

_____

_____

Name: _____

What Do Scientists Do?

Scientists try to find out how things work and why things happen. They ask questions and try different ways to answer them. They are very curious!

What kinds of questions do scientists ask? All kinds! They might wonder how Earth was made or why the sky is blue. Some ask how fish breathe in water or how the human body protects itself from diseases. Others might think about how we get energy from the Sun.

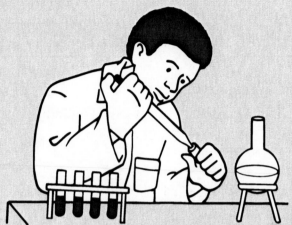

How do scientists try to answer their questions? They observe things. This means that they use their senses. They look with their eyes and listen with their ears. They record what they observe. They do tests. They use tools to measure how big, fast, or hot things are. Then, they use their observations to try to answer their questions.

When scientists think they have an answer to a question, they share it. They tell other scientists about what they found. They write about it. Science is not a secret! Other scientists can try the same tests to see if they answer the question the same way.

1. Scientists try to answer questions by _____.
   a. observing things   **b.** doing tests   **c.** both **a** and **b**

2. When scientists think they have the answer, they _____

_____.

3. As a scientist, what questions would you ask?

_____

_____

_____

Name: _____

Branches of Science

All scientists ask questions and look for answers. But not all scientists are curious about the same things. There are many different kinds of science!

Life Science is the study of living things.
- ➡ Some life scientists study plants or animals.
- ➡ Others study humans and medicine.

Physical Science is the study of energy and matter.
- ➡ Some scientists study energy, motion, and forces.
- ➡ Others study very small things that you can't see, such as atoms.

Earth and Space Science is the study of Earth and space.
- ➡ Some scientists study Earth's land and oceans.
- ➡ Some scientists study planets and stars.

Did You Know?

Some scientists mix together more than one kind of science. Paleontologists study things that lived long ago. Some study dinosaurs. They must know about life science to understand how animals and plants lived. They also know about Earth science so they can find and dig up fossils.

1. Life science is the study of _____.
   a. living things   **b.** nonliving things   **c.** things in space

2. Name three things that physical scientists study.

   _____   _____   _____

3. Would you rather study Earth or other planets? _____

   _____

   Explain why.

   _____

   _____

   _____

Name: _____

Data Measurement

When scientists want to answer a question, they do an experiment or a test. They **record** or write down what they observe. The things they write down are called **data**. Scientists look at the data after an experiment to see if they can answer the question they were testing.

I want to know if more birds will come to a wooden bird feeder or a plastic bird feeder. I put two cups of birdseed in each feeder. I hang the feeders from a tree. I observe the feeders for one hour.

1. What should I observe and record to answer my question?

_____

Taz and Mikela want to know if sunlight helps plants grow. They get two plants. They put one near the window where it will get lots of sun. They put one in a closet where it will not get any sun. They wait one week.

2. What data should they measure to answer their question?

_____

3. Circle the tool they should use to measure.

  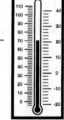

Shelby wants to know which toy car will roll the farthest. She sends the red car down the ramp. Then, she sends the blue car down the ramp.

4. What should Shelby measure to answer her question?

_____

5. Circle the tool she should use to measure.

Tilda wonders if hot chocolate cools off faster in a smaller cup. She puts hot chocolate in three cups of different sizes. She leaves them to cool for half an hour.

6. What should Tilda measure to answer her question?

_____

7. Circle the tool she should use to measure.

Name: _____

Interpreting Data

When scientists do an experiment, they observe what happens and write it down. The information they write down is called **data**. Scientists look at the data after an experiment. They use the data to try to answer the question they were testing.

Cass and George want to know what kind of liquid melts an ice cube the fastest. They get four different liquids. They pour each one into a separate cup. They drop an ice cube into each cup. All ice cubes started out the same size. After two minutes, they take the ice cubes out of the liquids. They measure the length of each ice cube.

Here is their data:

Liquid	Length of Ice Cube
water	2 cm
juice	5 cm
soda	4 cm
milk	4 cm

1. Finish the graph to show the results of this experiment. Use the *data* from the table above.

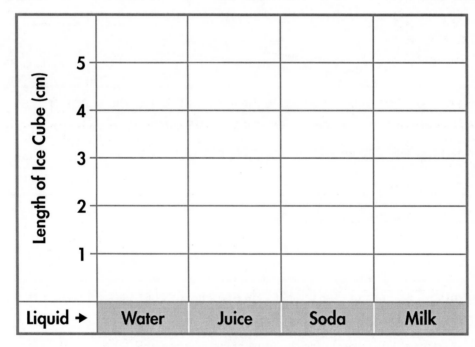

2. Which liquid made the ice cube melt the fastest? _____

How do you know? _____

What is your evidence? _____

_____

Name: _____

Measuring Data

When scientists do experiments, they sometimes need to measure things. Help the scientists with their measurements.

Professor Medina is studying the weather. She needs to know how cold it is outside.

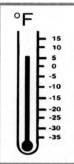

1. What is the temperature on the thermometer?

_____

Doctor Stacey is studying mice. He needs to know how long each mouse's tail is. Use the ruler to find the measurement.

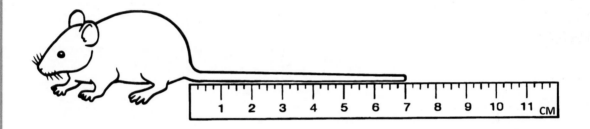

2. How many centimeters long is this mouse's tail? _____ cm

Ayden needs to use an exact amount of water in an experiment.

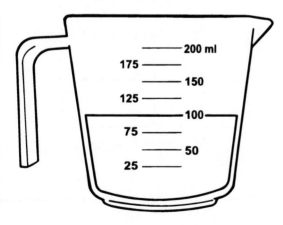

3. How much water is in the cup?

_____

Nidhi is studying cheetahs. She wants to know how fast they can run. She times them with a stopwatch.

4. How many seconds are shown on her stopwatch?

_____

Tracking Sheet

Unit 1 (pages 6–10)		Unit 8 (pages 41–45)		Unit 15 (pages 76–80)	
Why Do Animals Live in Groups?		When Habitats Change		What Is Force?	
Lion Prides		Raccoons and Habitat Change		Force and Motion	
Termite Homes		Save the Ferrets!		What Is Motion?	
A Termite Colony		Help the Warblers!		Force and Shape	
Ring-tailed Lemur Groups		Natural or Manmade Change?		Strength of Forces	

Unit 2 (pages 11–15)		Unit 9 (pages 46–50)		Unit 16 (pages 81–85)	
Why Animals Communicate		What Is a Fossil?		Balanced and Unbalanced Forces	
How Animals Share Information		How Do Fossils Form?		Unbalanced Forces	
Animals Communicate with Humans		What Can Fossils Tell Us?		Gravity	
Communicate with an Animal		Paleontologists		Gravity and Weight	
Can Plants Communicate?		The Fossil Record		Balancing Gravity	

Unit 3 (pages 16–20)		Unit 10 (pages 51–55)		Unit 17 (pages 86–90)	
Animal Life Cycles		What Is Weather?		Friction	
Animals: Birth and Growth		Weather Can Change		Friction and Motion	
Mammal Life Cycles		Types of Weather		Air Resistance	
Reptile and Amphibian Life Cycles		Dangerous Weather		Interpreting Data: Friction	
Insect Life Cycles		Weather Activity		The Feather and the Hammer	

Unit 4 (pages 21–25)		Unit 11 (pages 56–60)		Unit 18 (pages 91–95)	
Inherited Traits		Weather Forecasting		Magnets	
Traits Change Over Time		Meteorologists		North and South Poles	
Acquired Traits		Weather Tools		Attract or Repel?	
Inherited or Acquired?		Fun with Forecasting		What Is Magnetic?	
The Best of Its Kind		Read the Weather Forecast		Magnets Can Do Work	

Unit 5 (pages 26–30)		Unit 12 (pages 61–65)		Unit 19 (pages 96–100)	
What Are Biomes?		What Is Hazardous Weather?		Sir Isaac Newton	
Nonliving Parts of Biomes		Severe Thunderstorms		Newton's First Law of Motion	
Interpreting Graphs: Biomes		Winter Storms		Newton's Second Law of Motion	
Biome Plants		Heat Waves and Drought		Newton's Third Law of Motion	
Ecosystems		Preparing for Weather Hazards		Observe, Measure, and Predict Force	

Unit 6 (pages 31–35)		Unit 13 (pages 66–70)		Unit 20 (pages 101–105)	
Physical Adaptations to Get Food		Climate vs. Weather		What Do Scientists Do?	
Physical Adaptations for Protection		Climate or Weather?		Branches of Science	
Physical Adaptations to Stay Warm or Cool		Temperature and Precipitation		Data Measurement	
Physical Adaptations of Plants		Climate Zones		Interpreting Data	
Invent an Animal		Climate Data		Measuring Data	

Unit 7 (pages 36–40)		Unit 14 (pages 71–75)	
Instincts for Getting Food		States of Matter	
Learned Behaviors for Getting Food		Solids	
Behaviors to Stay Safe		Liquids	
Behaviors to Stay Warm or Cool		Gases	
Behaviors in Plants		Phase Changes	

Answer Key

Unit 1—Animal Groups

Why Do Animals Live in Groups? (page 6)
1. benefits
2. Any 3: birds, elephants, wolves, meerkats, mule deer
3. One animal can warn others of danger; animals can share work

Lion Prides (page 7)
1. a pride
2. It is easier to catch prey when they help one another; they help one another take care of the cubs
3. Check for appropriate answers.

Termite Homes (page 8)
1. b
2. queen, worker, soldier
3. to protect one another

A Termite Colony (page 9)
1. c
2. Worker termites build the nest and feed the other termites.
3. No, because it would not be able to build a nest by itself. It would not have soldiers to defend it.

Ring-tailed Lemur Groups (page 10)
1. Check that bar graph matches data.
2. Ando's
3. Linah's
4. 6 more lemurs

Unit 2—Living Things Communicate

Why Animals Communicate (page 11)
1. a
2. Check for appropriate answers.
3. Check for appropriate answers.

How Animals Share Information (page 12)
1. b
2. Students should mention sound, touch, or smell.
3. Check for appropriate answers.

Animals Communicate with Humans (page 13)
1. a
2. b
3. Because it wants honey.

Communicate with an Animal (page 14)
1–5. Check for appropriate answers and drawings.

Can Plants Communicate? (page 15)
1. by releasing chemicals
2. Chemical messages travel by air or through the plant's roots.
3. a

Unit 3—Animal Life Cycles

Animal Life Cycles (page 16)
1. a
2. Hatch from an egg; born alive
3. There wouldn't be any more animals.

Animals: Birth and Growth (page 17)
1. b
2. alligator, dog (puppy), people (humans); accept other correct answers
3. Check for appropriate answers.

Mammal Life Cycles (page 18)
1. Check for appropriate answers.
2. A-3, B-1, C-4, D-2

Reptile and Amphibian Life Cycles (page 19)
1. They find sunlight to warm themselves up.
2. Review organizer for appropriate answers.
   Amphibians: babies do not look like parents
   Both: cold blooded; need sun to warm up
   Reptiles: babies look like parents when born or hatched

Insect Life Cycles (page 20)
1. egg, nymph, adult
2. egg, larva, pupa, adult

Unit 4—Traits

Inherited Traits (page 21)
1. a
2. Check for appropriate answers.
3. Check for appropriate answers.
4. Check for appropriate answers.

Traits Change Over Time (page 22)
1. c
2. b
3. Some of their traits come from their mother and some from their father, so they could each get some different traits.

Acquired Traits (page 23)
1. a
2. c
3. Check for appropriate answers.

Inherited or Acquired? (page 24)
Inherited: eye color, size of ears
Acquired: eating with a fork, scars, language spoken
Both: skin color, playing piano

Answer Key (cont.)

The Best of Its Kind (page 25)
1. b 2. b 3. c
4. Check for appropriate answers.

Unit 5—Biomes and Ecosystems

What Are Biomes? (page 26)
1. b
2. grasslands
3. The marine region has salty water and the freshwater region has fresh water.

Nonliving Parts of Biomes (page 27)
1. a
2. c
3. Check for appropriate answers.

Interpreting Graphs: Biomes (page 28)
1. 110°F; 75°F; 35°F
2. 1 inch
3. The desert biome, because it has high temperatures and very little rain.
4. 85°; 80°; 5°
5. Site B gets a lot of rain each month.
6. The forest, because the temperatures are always warm and there is a lot of rain.

Biome Plants (page 29)
1. grassland 3. forest 5. aquatic
2. desert 4. tundra

Ecosystems (page 30)
1. Since black bears hibernate, they must live in deciduous forests where the winters are cold.
2. Because boa constrictors are cold-blooded, they must live in the rainforest where it is warm all the time.

Unit 6—Physical Adaptations

Physical Adaptations to Get Food (page 31)
1. c
2. Spoonbills probably live in a habitat with shallow water because they walk in the water and swish their beaks.
3. Crossbills live in a habitat with pine trees because they eat seeds from pinecones.
4. A spoonbill could not survive in a crossbill's habitat because it could not find food in pine trees. It needs shallow water.

Physical Adaptations for Protection (page 32)
1. b
2. a
3. They can run very fast.
4. b

Physical Adaptations to Stay Warm or Cool (page 33)
1. c
2. It has a thick layer of fat, or blubber.
3. Foxes have large ears to cool off. Ostriches do not have feathers on their heads, necks, or legs. This helps them cool off. Polar bears have black skin and blubber.

Physical Adaptations of Plants (page 34)
1. b
2. leaves, roots
3. No, because it cannot survive in the cold. It is adapted for the hot desert.

Invent an Animal (page 35)
1–4. Check for appropriate answers.

Unit 7—Behavioral Adaptations

Instincts for Getting Food (page 36)
1. a
2. Because they cannot find food in the winter.
3. It is something an animal knows how to do without being taught.

Learned Behaviors for Getting Food (page 37)
1. c
2. They might die. They might move lower down the mountain where food is easier to find.
3. Check for appropriate answers.

Behaviors to Stay Safe (page 38)
1. a
2. b
3. sounds
4. Check for appropriate answers. *Example:* Look both ways before crossing the street.

Behaviors to Stay Warm or Cool (page 39)
1. c
2. To keep warm; because they cannot find food in winter
3. Check for appropriate answers. *Examples:* Put on warm clothes; stay inside where it is warmer

Behaviors in Plants (page 40)
Check for appropriate answers.

Unit 8—When Habitats Change

When Habitats Change (page 41)
1. a
2. Check for appropriate answers.
3. They can adapt and survive, they can move to a new place, or they can die.

Answer Key *(cont.)*

Raccoons and Habitat Change (page 42)

1. b
2. c
3. Check for appropriate answers.

Save the Ferrets! (page 43)

1. a
2. food and shelter
3. People built farms and cities on the grasslands. There weren't enough prairie dogs for the ferrets to eat.

Help the Warblers! (page 44)

1. c
2. b
3. restoring the warbler habitat by planting new Ashe juniper trees

Natural or Manmade Change? (page 45)

1. Natural
2. Manmade
3. Natural
4. Natural
5. Manmade
6. Manmade

Unit 9—Fossils

What Is a Fossil? (page 46)

1. b
2. body fossils, trace fossils
3. Check for appropriate answers.

How Do Fossils Form? (page 47)

1. To decay means to break into tiny pieces and become part of the dirt.
2. b
3. No, a jellyfish cannot become a body fossil because it has no hard body parts.

What Can Fossils Tell Us? (page 48)

1. c
2. how animals lived and what the land was like
3. Fossils found in lower layers of rock lived longer ago than fossils in higher layers. Fossils found in the same layer probably lived at the same time.

Paleontologists (page 49)

1. c
2. Any three: digs them up carefully; measures them; photographs and draws them; cleans them and studies them; writes about them; shares information.
3. Check for appropriate answers.

The Fossil Record (page 50)

1. how living things have changed over millions of years
2. Any two: Not many living things became fossils; we find very few fossils; paleontologists sometimes make mistakes
3. They change their ideas to fit the new evidence.

Unit 10—What Is Weather?

What Is Weather? (page 51)

1. b
2. precipitation
3. Check for appropriate answers.

Weather Can Change (page 52)

1. is not
2. Earth tilts slightly towards the Sun part of the time and slightly away from the Sun the rest of the time. This causes the days to be shorter or longer and the weather to be warmer or colder.
3. Check for appropriate answers.

Types of Weather (page 53)

1. a
2. warm air and cold air bump into one another
3. Check for appropriate answers.

Dangerous Weather (page 54)

1. c
2. Any two: water, wind, electricity
3. *Possible answers:* A hurricane can move cars and ruin buildings. It can push waves to the shore. It can cause flooding.

Weather Activity (page 55)
Check for appropriate answers for each type of weather.

Unit 11—Weather Forecasting

Weather Forecasting (page 56)

1. b
2. c
3. Check for appropriate answers.

Meteorologists (page 57)

1. c
2. patterns in the weather
3. Check for appropriate answers.

Weather Tools (page 58)

1. b
2. a
3. the amount of rain that falls, temperature, wind speed and direction
4. where storms are; how much rain, snow, and wind are in an area; which direction storms are moving and how fast

Fun with Forecasting (page 59)

1. a
2. Look to see if the pinecones are open or closed. If the pinecones are closed, it may rain. If the pinecones are open, it should be a nice day.
3. $43 + 37 = 80°$

Answer Key (cont.)

Read the Weather Forecast (page 60)

1. 62°
2. Tuesday
3. Friday because it will be windy.
4. Saturday
5. Cooler, because the temperature keeps dropping.
6. No because it will be raining.
7. Something warm.

Unit 12—Weather Hazards

What Is Hazardous Weather? (page 61)

1. b
2. c
3. Check for appropriate answers.

Severe Thunderstorms (page 62)

1. a
2. stay indoors
3. They can destroy buildings and throw large objects up into the air.

Winter Storms (page 63)

1. c
2. stay indoors and try to keep warm
3. Check for appropriate answers.

Heat Waves and Drought (page 64)

1. a
2. stay indoors and try to keep cool
3. Check for appropriate answers.

Preparing for Weather Hazards (page 65)

1. a
2. Any two: build dams and channels, build houses on stilts, use sand bags to keep water out
3. Check for appropriate answers.

Unit 13—What Is Climate?

Climate vs. Weather (page 66)

1. c
2. the pattern of weather in a place over a long time. Example: Check for appropriate answers.
3. Check for appropriate answers.

Climate or Weather? (page 67)

1. W	3. C	5. C	7. W	9. W
2. W	4. W	6. C	8. C	10. W

Temperature and Precipitation (page 68)

1. b
2. how hot or cold the air feels
3. patterns in temperature and precipitation

Climate Zones (page 69)

1. a
2. Because the Sun shines a long time each day, all year long.
3. Check for appropriate answers.

Climate Data (page 70)

1.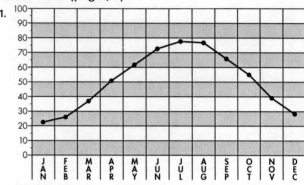

2. 55 degrees
3. Temperate Zone, because it is warm in summer and cold in winter.

Unit 14—States of Matter

States of Matter (page 71)

1. They stay close together and don't move around.
2. They stay close together, but they move around.
3. They spread apart and move in all directions.

Solids (page 72)

1. b
2. shape
3. Check for appropriate answers.

Liquids (page 73)

1. c
2. Check for appropriate answers.
3. The particles stay close together, but they can move around.

Gases (page 74)

1. a
2. mixture
3. The gas will spread out into the air.

Phase Changes (page 75)

1. cookie – solid   rain – liquid
   a sponge – solid   oxygen – gas
   water vapor – gas   shampoo – liquid
2. melts
   evaporates
   freezes
3. The soda is liquid. The bubbles are gas. The ice is solid.

Answer Key (cont.)

Unit 15—What Is Force?

What Is Force? (page 76)

1. a force that moves something away
2. Check for appropriate answers.
3. a force that moves something closer
4. Check for appropriate answers.

Force and Motion (page 77)

1. b
2. force
3. Any two: start moving, stop moving, speed up, slow down, change direction

What Is Motion? (page 78)

1. c
2. It changes position.
3. Check for appropriate answers. Possible responses include snails and clock hands.
4. Check for appropriate answers.

Force and Shape (page 79)

1. c
2. force
3. Check for appropriate answers.

Strength of Forces (page 80)

1. b
2. c
3. Check for appropriate answers.
4. Check for appropriate answers.

Unit 16—Balanced and Unbalanced Forces

Balanced and Unbalanced Forces (page 81)

1. balanced
2. unbalanced
3. strength; opposite

Unbalanced Forces (page 82)

1. The forces are *unbalanced* because the mower is moving.
2. The forces are *balanced* because the kid is not moving.
3. The forces are *unbalanced* because the ball is moving.
4. The forces are *balanced* because the kids are not moving.

Gravity (page 83)

1. b
2. Earth is very big.
3. the center of the planet

Gravity and Weight (page 84)

1. b
2. less or weaker
3. a measurement of how strongly gravity is pulling on something
4. The pull of the Moon's gravity is less than the pull of Earth's gravity.

Balancing Gravity (page 85)

1. a
2. b
3. The force of gravity is pulling down and the desk is pushing up with the same amount of force. The forces are balanced.

Unit 17—Friction and Air Resistance

Friction (page 86)

1. b
2. a
3. Check for appropriate answers.

Friction and Motion (page 87)

1. b
2. opposite
3. tile; Check for appropriate answers.

Air Resistance (page 88)

1. c
2. the air

3–4. Check the arrows and the labels.

Interpreting Data: Friction (page 89)

1. tile
2. carpet
3. 21 inches
4. tile; the car traveled farthest on tile.

The Feather and the Hammer (page 90)

1. a
2. No, a parachute would not be needed because there is no air so there is no air resistance to slow them down.
3. Check for appropriate answers.

Unit 18—Magnets

Magnets (page 91)

1. a
2. attracted
3. repelled
4. attracting; repelling

North and South Poles (page 92)

1. b
2. They will repel or push away from one another.
3. South
4. North

Answer Key (cont.)

Attract or Repel? (page 93)

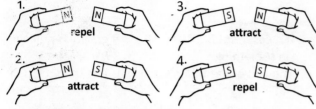

What Is Magnetic? (page 94)

Magnets Can Do Work (page 95)
1. Check for appropriate answers.
2. to see what is wrong when someone is sick
3. to collect the metal that cows eat and to keep the cows healthy

Unit 19: Laws of Motion

Sir Isaac Newton (page 96)
1. b
2. newtons
3. Check for appropriate answers.

Newton's First Law of Motion (page 97)
1. a
2. gravity, friction, air resistance
3. Check for appropriate answers.

Newton's Second Law of Motion (page 98)
1. c
2. No, because it would only go a short distance.
3. The soccer ball will move faster because it has less mass than the bowling ball.

Newton's Third Law of Motion (page 99)
1. a

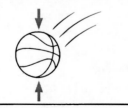

2. _____
3. As your foot pushes back, the skateboard goes in the opposite direction.

Observe, Measure, and Predict Force (page 100)
1. ←
2. ↑
3. Check for appropriate answers.

Unit 20—About Science

What Do Scientists Do? (page 101)
1. c
2. share it
3. Check for appropriate answers.

Branches of Science (page 102)
1. a
2. Any three: energy, matter, motion, forces, atoms
3. Check appropriate answers.

Data Measurement (page 103)
1. the number of birds that come to each feeder
2. the height of the plants
3. yardstick/ruler
4. the distance each car rolls
5. measuring tape
6. the temperature of the hot chocolate in each cup
7. thermometer

Interpreting Data (page 104)

1.
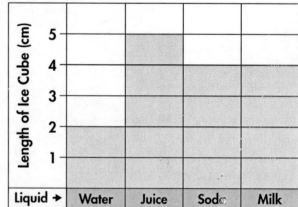

2. The water made the ice cube melt the fastest because when they measured the ice cubes the one in the water shows the shortest bar.

Measuring Data (page 105)
1. 5°F
2. 7 cm
3. 100 ml
4. 20 seconds